A NEW CHINA POLICY

Some Quaker Proposals

A NEW CHINA POLICY

SOME QUAKER PROPOSALS

A Report Prepared for the

American Friends Service Committee

New Haven and London, Yale University Press, 1965

Copyright © 1965 by Yale University.
Designed by John O. C. McCrillis,
set in Garamond type,
and printed in the United States of America by
the Carl Purington Rollins Printing-Office
of the Yale University Press, New Haven, Connecticut.
Jacket design by Guy M. de Lesseps.
Distributed in Canada by McGill University Press.

Library of Congress catalog card number: 65–15048

FOREWORD

The United States and the People's Republic of China have become almost completely separated by a wall of mutual hostility. There is no cultural exchange, no trade, no intervisitation, and no diplomatic contact except for occasional official encounters in off-the-record talks at Warsaw. There has been no settlement of the Korean War, only a cease-fire. Contact between Chinese and Americans is still "dealing with the enemy." China views our military installations near its borders and our support of the Nationalist government on Taiwan as aggression. The United States considers them to be justifiable defense against the spread of Communism in Asia. While the people of the United States are too little aware of the situation, the people of China are almost daily confronted with posters or broadcasts picturing the United States as imperialist, and as the enemy preventing the unification of China and Taiwan. The United States has become *the* enemy; fear and hatred of our country help bind the Chinese people of the mainland together.

This is an atmosphere of war, not peace. As members of the Society of Friends (Quakers), we believe that men can resolve their differences without violence or the threat of violence. But the peaceful unity of mankind requires a sense of brotherhood based on mutual understanding which is now lacking between China and the United States. We believe that the present situation is dangerous as well as tragic, not just for ourselves and the Chinese but for the entire world.

Our report on the China policy of the United States is written in the hope that, speaking out of Quaker experience with China, we may contribute to better understanding and more hopeful policy approaches. In past years, the Society of Friends has had strong ties with Chinese of the mainland—in West China, in the Nanking area, and in the university centers of Canton and Peking. Groups of Chinese Quakers developed and many strong friendships were formed. During and after World War II, the Friends Ambulance Unit, in which more than 150 conscientious objectors participated, trucked medical supplies, provided medical teams, rehabilitated hospitals, and carried on relief projects both in areas controlled by the Nationalist government and in areas under Chinese Communist control. Since 1950, Friends have continued to work in Taiwan and Hong Kong. To us, the Chinese are not a great mass of unknown beings, but people with human strengths and weaknesses like our own.

This report on United States–China relations is one of a series of similar reports which the American Friends Service Committee has issued, the first of which was *The United States and the Soviet Union* in 1949. Following this came *Steps to Peace* in 1952, and *Speak Truth to Power* in 1955. Each of these has been the work of a special study group. Throughout this report, the problems of international relations and world peace, and particularly of relations between the United States and the People's Republic of China, are treated only in part as political and military problems. They are also approached from an ethical, humanitarian, and religious point of view. As members of the Society of Friends (Quakers), the authors affirm the concern for peace which has always been one of the fundamentals of Quakerism. This striving for a peaceful world follows from a belief in the oneness of mankind and the worth of each person.

Callousness toward individuals and groups of peoples tends to increase with the power to destroy. It is essential, therefore, that we bend every effort toward preserving, not destroying, human life; toward enhancing, not degrading it. As Pope John XXIII stated in his *Pacem in Terris*, "Every human being is a person . . . [with] rights and duties of his own, flowing directly and simultaneously from his very nature; which rights are therefore universal, inviolable and inalienable."[1]

Friends, too, affirm a way of life which holds each human being to be of great value, not to be used as a means to an end or to be destroyed, but rather to be respected and assured the basic rights of self-fulfillment. In the past, these convictions have involved members of the Society of Friends in such pioneering as William

1. *Pacem in Terris,* Encyclical Letter of Pope John XXIII (New York, American Press, 1963), p. 5.

Penn's establishment of Pennsylvania in 1682 as a "Holy Experiment," and his treaties with the Indians. Friends were also early activists in prison reform, in treatment of the mentally ill by nonviolent means, and, nearly a century before the Civil War, in the freeing of their own slaves and working for emancipation of all slaves. By conviction and by tradition, Friends have stood among the advocates of human rights, the reconcilers, the peacemakers, the restorers of broken communications.

Today Friends continue to create opportunities for service in the cause of peace, both as individuals and as members of Quaker organizations such as the American Friends Service Committee. The Service Committee was founded during the First World War to open ways for young conscientious objectors to help relieve suffering and assist in reconstruction. It has continued to be active, working in many parts of the United States and abroad, engaging in a wide variety of projects. Though well known as a relief agency, its fundamental aim is and always has been the promotion of peace between people of different races, different nations, and different ideologies.

The Board of Directors of the American Friends Service Committee, concerned for the restoration of communication between American and Chinese, invited us to serve as a working party to prepare a report dealing with U.S.–China relations. This paper is the result. We have undertaken to speak essentially from a Quaker point of view, believing that questions of policy must be considered in terms of ethical and human values as well as in terms of economic interest and political power. We believe that economics and politics cannot be divorced from morals and religious conviction, for these are matters that affect the lives and welfare of people; therefore they can be resolved only by taking into account the dignity and worth of persons, the power of active goodwill, and the practical relevance of spiritual resources which we believe are working among all men for good.

We are a diverse group: scholars, businessmen, some with long experience in the Orient, men and women familiar with public opinion and others with experience in the perplexing dilemmas of government service. We sought unity in our deliberations rather than uniformity. As with any multi-author document, there remained differences of approach, emphasis, and style as well as judgment. But there was agreement on the basic and urgent need for a change in American policy to help restore communication with the Chinese.

The primary purpose of this study, therefore, is to examine the many problems underlying the present relationships between the United States and the People's Republic of China. We hope to promote clearer thinking so that we and those who share our concern may be able better to encourage action on these issues and to contribute to the creation of a climate in which the United States can move toward more fruitful policies. The magnitude of the problem is overwhelming, and its ramifications are extensive. No short or easy answers can be expected. However, we believe that moral and spiritual insights are relevant, even in difficulties as great as these.

MEMBERS OF THE
WORKING PARTY ON CHINA POLICY
AMERICAN FRIENDS SERVICE COMMITTEE
SEPTEMBER 1964–FEBRUARY 1965

LEWIS M. HOSKINS, *Convenor*

Jackson H. Bailey
Eugene Boardman
Hugh Borton
Kenneth Boulding
Robert Cory
William Hanson
Timothy Haworth
Halleck Hoffman
Michael Ingerman
J. Stuart Innerst
Stewart Meacham
Rhoads Murphey
Esther Rhoads
Benjamin Seaver
Dorothy Gilbert Thorne

CONTENTS

CONTENTS

1. ORIGINS OF THE PRESENT IMPASSE

"Governments, as well as courts, change their fashions," said William Penn; "the same clothes will not always serve. And politics made obsolete by new accidents are as unsafe to follow as antiquated clothes are ridiculous to wear."[2]

Since 1950, the United States and the government of mainland China have adopted policies which stand like a great wall between the two nations, preventing all normal contacts. Conditions are set, policies remain largely unchanged, and hostility increases. The two nations are enemies. They do not speak to one another, except occasionally at the ambassadorial level at Warsaw.

Meanwhile the world moves on; everywhere there are tremendous changes. "New accidents" make old "politics" or policies obsolete. The great acceleration in communication and transportation, the emergence of new nations seeking patterns for development, changes within the Soviet Union, changes within China, changes within the United States, changes in the international scene in general, the vast proliferation of atomic power, and the increased destructiveness of modern weaponry—all these call for a new approach. Even before China exploded its first nuclear device in October 1964 these developments made it unsafe for the United States and the People's Republic of China to follow their old policies toward one another.

The problems created by the inflexible attitudes of both of these two powerful nations are potentially dangerous. Through the relentless, skillful, and tireless efforts of the Chinese Communists under the leadership of Mao Tse-tung, the People's Republic of China has become one of the world's greatest powers. Its control and governance of mainland China, comprising nearly one-fourth of the world's population, is firmly established and its special form of communism has permeated Chinese society.

2. *The Quaker Reader,* ed. Jessamyn West (New York, Viking Press, 1962), p. 216.

Nowhere in the world have there been more dynamic and drastic changes than in the emerging new China. The ancient social and political order of traditional China has been largely overthrown, and many millions of Chinese have given themselves with enormous zeal to the revolutionary transformation of their country. Within a generation, China has absorbed much of modern technology and has gained the status of a great power. It has given the physical well-being of its people a high priority on its agenda of national renewal by an intensive program of medical care and public health. Among other revolutionary changes are the elevation of the status of women, a nationwide effort to stamp out illiteracy, and the planning of a coeducational program from the kindergarten through college.

By 1965 the new China had expanded its trade to include more than 100 nations. Trade with noncommunist countries in 1964 exceeded two billion U.S. dollars worth of goods. China has challenged the Soviet Union's leadership in the Communist world. It displayed its military prowess in Korea. It is recognized by or has diplomatic relations with more than 50 countries. It has established its influence and authority in peripheral areas which, during the periods of China's imperial power, traditionally have been under Chinese dominance in varying degrees; and it is continuing to assert itself in such areas. Whatever one's attitude toward the changes that have taken place, the policy of the United States toward China must meet the new situation created by these developments. It is time, indeed, that the United States adopted a new approach to China which can, in the long run, evoke a new response. Both Americans and Chinese need to take into account certain aspects of our present and past situations which will affect future relationships.

TWO SEPARATE CULTURES

There have never been entirely easy relations between China and Western countries. This situation is a product of geographical isolation and the attainment independently of high levels of culture in both China and the West. Imperial China's system of diplomatic relations treated all foreign nations as tribute-bearing inferiors. The "unequal treaties" which the Western countries later forced upon China were based upon a Western attitude of

U.N. MEMBER STATES WHICH HAVE DIPLOMATIC RELATIONS WITH COMMUNIST CHINA (49)

Afghanistan	France	Romania
Albania	Ghana	Senegal
Algeria	Guinea	Somalia
Bulgaria	Hungary	Sudan
Burma	India	Sweden
Burundi	Iraq	Syria
Byelorussian S.S.R.	Israel	Tanzania
Cambodia	Kenya	Tunisia
Central African	Laos	Uganda
Republic	Mali	Ukrainian S.S.R.
Ceylon	Mongolia	U.S.S.R.
Congo (Brazzaville)	Morocco	U.A.R.
Cuba	Nepal	United Kingdom
Czechoslovakia	Netherlands	Yemen
Dahomey	Norway	Yugoslavia
Denmark	Pakistan	Zambia
Finland	Poland	

COUNTRIES OUTSIDE THE U.N. WHICH HAVE DIPLOMATIC RELATIONS WITH COMMUNIST CHINA

East Germany	North Korea	Switzerland
Indonesia	North Vietnam	

superiority and were accompanied by humiliating disabilities. They were removed only in 1943 when these treaties were finally ended. Unable to defend itself or to raise adequate capital for development, China was saddled with indemnities and long-term debts to Western governments and bankers. After 1949 China emerged from civil war with a system of foreign relations that divided the world into friends and enemies and established separate procedures for dealing with each. It assumed that continuing struggle would persist into the indefinite future. China's foreign relations today bear the mark of these experiences.

Communications between the United States or any Western country and China are vexed by the fact that China and the West represent two great but different streams of human history which have only recently come into major contact. The Han Empire of China and the Roman Empire each knew vaguely that the other was there, but there was no direct contact. Buddhism came from India and made a substantial impact on China, Korea, and Japan, although it was largely transformed in the process. China made no corresponding impact on India. In spite of occasional trips like that of Marco Polo in the thirteenth century, European awareness of China dates mainly from the eighteenth century when the impact of China on Europe was substantial. Chinese influence in furniture and architecture and even dress became fashionable. The whole idea of a state ruled by scholars and gentlemen made a profound impression upon European thought of the Enlightenment.

Until then, these two broad streams of culture, one coming from Mount Sinai, the Acropolis, Jerusalem, and Rome, the other growing up in East Asia, were so separate that little knowledge and no concern were shared. China knew nothing of Aristotle, Moses, Jesus, Mohammed, Thomas Aquinas, Galileo, Newton, or others whom the West regards as the architects of a true and good life. On the other hand, the great names in China's culture—Confucius, Laotze, Han Wu-ti, Ssu-ma, Ch'ien, Li Po, or Wang An-shih—to this day mean little in the West. China, Korea, and Japan produced a civilization as rich aesthetically and technologically as that of the West, until the end of the eighteenth century. In that century, indeed, Adam Smith could regard China as the summit of economic achievement, the country where economic development had gone as far as it possibly could and had been stabilized.

Nevertheless the nineteenth century was an era of cumulative disaster and calamity for China. Dynastic decline, economic distress, civil war, repeated defeat and encroachment at the hands of foreign nations, and stubborn ethnocentric resistance to change left China weak and unready for the demands of modern civilization. By 1900 China's leaders, faced with the bleak results of resistance to change over the previous 60 years, felt forced to question every feature of their proud civilization. Efforts during the subsequent 50 years to reform, to modernize, and to make their country adequate to the Western challenge largely failed. The Chinese Communists felt that they had to make up for these failures. In their minds were also the achievements of the great

4

Chinese empires of the past, such as the Han, the T'ang, and the Ch'ing. They had to convert their country swiftly into a modern nation, and at the same time equal or surpass the great empires of the past. The drastic measures, the stridency, and the fierce energy of the past 15 years are not simply the expression of Communist ideas and methods.

In the nineteenth and twentieth centuries, the two great streams of human culture described above met in a single channel, where they now flow side by side, at present with little mingling, as the Arve and Rhone flow in a single channel without mingling below Geneva. Mingle they eventually must, but we must not be surprised if 4000 years in separate historical watersheds make it difficult for the waters to mix and for communication to take place.

AMERICAN POLICY TO 1949

Relations between the United States and China since the beginnings of American trade with the Chinese Empire have passed through widely differing phases. Until the first Anglo-Chinese War (1839–42)—often referred to as the Opium War—China was in control of the forms of its trade and diplomatic relations with the rest of the world. But from 1844 to 1943 these were governed by a set of treaties that gave special privileges to Western nations and limited China's sovereignty by granting extraterritoriality, a treaty tariff, special concessions of land, and various development rights. China became a semi-colony of the West, and the Chinese remember the period as one of national humiliation.

At the same time, the United States, despite the terms of a Sino-American treaty which called for reciprocity, by domestic legislation in the 1880s excluded Chinese as immigrants. The United States acted in concert with other Western powers in using treaty privileges to expand trade and cultural and religious activities; on the other hand during the same period many Americans developed feelings of warmth and affection for the Chinese and many contributed funds and leadership to projects for the improvement of physical, social, and educational conditions. In the late 1890s, influenced by British advice, Americans launched the Open Door Policy, which called for equal commercial privileges for all nations in China and for noninfringement on China's territory and sovereignty. However naïvely, this policy reflected our goodwill toward China and our opposition to any territorial aggrandizement there, as well as American determination to share in economic opportunities secured by other countries.

The United States was instrumental in having the Open Door as a diplomatic policy imbedded in the Washington Conference Nine-Power Treaty of 1922, but did not implement it with international legal machinery. It refused to join the League of Nations. With other Western powers, it also showed little interest in helping Sun Yat-sen, the leader of the Chinese revolutionary movement, to strengthen his political party, the Kuomintang, and to push forward the unification of China. In the 1920s, he turned for support to Russia and the newly formed Chinese Communist Party. Resentment of the U.S. attitude was shared by a broad spectrum of Chinese leadership. Although the United States was committed to preserve China's "territorial and administrative integrity" throughout this period, when Japan attacked Manchuria in 1931 it acquiesced in Japanese militarism by continuing to sell Japan strategic materials, and gave little or no help to Nationalist China except for minor loans plus "moral support" by denouncing Japanese aggression. Japanese bombs made from American scrap iron hit mission properties in China built with American money.

During the 1930s, the United States continued to pay lip service to the Open Door Policy, but in fact acted in isolationist terms. This contributed to the combination of forces, including Japanese attack and internal disintegration, which destroyed much that was positive in Nationalist China and crippled the Kuomintang's ability to assume postwar leadership. American partnership with China, both Communist and Nationalist, in the defeat of Japan gave way in 1945 to our many-faceted support (just short of full military involvement) to the Nationalists in their struggle against the Communists. Involvement in the domestic quarrels of other countries is always a dangerous policy. In this case it proved disastrous, since we backed the losing side, prolonging the civil conflict and adding greatly to Chinese suffering. Communist China's fear and resentment of the United States is understandable.

By 1948 the Kuomintang (Nationalist) government was hopelessly demoralized. Faced with overwhelming reconstruction tasks after the devastating war, it could neither satisfy the needs of China

6

nor defend itself against the Communists. Its defeat in 1949 was soon followed by the withdrawal of all U.S. diplomatic representatives from the mainland. The Chinese people, considered by some as "the chief foreign recipient of our religious good will and good works . . . seemed in 1949 to have rejected us";[3] and for the better part of a year, until the beginning of the Korean War in June 1950, the United States government had little to do even with the Nationalist refugee government on Taiwan (Formosa), claiming in the China White Paper of 1949 that U.S. aid had been unavailing and our advice unheeded. Frustration over these events in China caused the "China Problem" to become a major issue in American politics. Many failed to see that the collapse of Nationalist leadership had by 1948 left the Chinese little alternative. The reaction in the United States was to seek a scapegoat: Americans who had "lost" or "given" China to the Communists. The irrelevance of such a frame of reference can be seen from this assessment of the impressions in 1945 of General Albert Wedemeyer, Chiang Kai-shek's chief of staff after General Stillwell's removal:

> Wedemeyer had the impression that the task faced by Chiang Kai-shek of bringing about stability and democracy in China was beyond his powers, as he thought they would be beyond those of any one man. For, among many reasons, the Generalissimo lacked able, honest advisers and assistants; he was surrounded by selfish and unscrupulous men; he was loyal to warlords and officials who had helped him in the past but who were now exploiting their position to enrich themselves and their families (only South Chinese had been appointed as governors and mayors in North China).[4]

After Communist Victory

When the Communists came to power in 1949, Americans were ill prepared psychologically to accept either the bankruptcy

3. John K. Fairbank, *Communist China and Taiwan in United States Foreign Policy,* The Brien McMahon Lectures (Storrs, University of Connecticut, 1960), pp. 7–8.

4. Herbert Feis, *The China Tangle* (Princeton, Princeton University Press, 1953), p. 400.

and defeat of the Nationalist regime of Chiang Kai-shek, which sought refuge on Taiwan, or the strength and dynamism of the Chinese People's Republic of Mao Tse-tung. In spite of this, by early 1950 the United States was preparing to recognize the new regime. Such action might well have been acceptable to the American people, especially in view of the support of John Foster Dulles, who suggested in his book *War or Peace,* published in the spring of 1950, that it would be wise to establish relations with the new government after its stability had "been tested over a reasonable period of time."[5]

However, all was changed when, at the outbreak of the Korean War, the U.S. Seventh Fleet was stationed in the Taiwan Straits. China's entry into the war five months later as U.S.-U.N. troops approached the Yalu River led to a different and completely hostile phase in Sino-American relations during which the Chinese People's Republic became the object of economic blockade, military confrontation, and thoroughgoing opposition as part of a U.S. "containment" policy. This policy assumed that communism was monolithic and that every move of Communist states was directed from Moscow. Step by step we extended military and economic support to Taiwan as an ally in the containment process. This involved us also in the Nationalist commitment to reconquest of the mainland.

Americans were told, and many have believed, that Chinese entry into the Korean War was an act of unprovoked aggression. To understand this action, though not to condone it, we must put ourselves in China's position. Since Korea had for centuries prior to the Japanese occupation been in effect a Chinese protectorate under the traditional imperial system, China's interest was more strongly involved than if Korea had been merely a neighboring country.[6] In addition, the Chinese entered the war only after they had made it clear that the approach of U.S.-U.N. armies to their own border would be resisted and warned the United States of their intentions. The battle was in fact on the

5. John Foster Dulles, *War or Peace* (New York, Macmillan, 1955), p. 190.

6. We are aware of the irony inherent in the role which imperialistic tradition seems to be playing in the life of China with its strictures against colonialism.

Chinese frontier and they themselves were directly threatened; Americans can get a sense of how it must have felt to the Chinese by imagining a reverse situation in Mexico. Under such circumstances we would undoubtedly regard the presence in Mexico of an advancing Chinese army as a danger to our security, especially if we had repeatedly warned the Chinese that we would feel obliged to attack them if they carried the battle near our border. The relevant fact is not whether in 1950 United Nations troops under MacArthur intended to cross the Yalu River into China after their sweep across the 38th parallel into North Korea, but rather whether the Chinese had reason to believe that there was such an intent.

The difficulties of communication are compounded by the fact that the leaders of China are now Marxists, and Marxists of a peculiarly doctrinaire and rigorous variety despite the fact that Marxism is a Western invention stamped indelibly with concepts of the Judeo-Christian tradition. Marx was a Jew, educated in a Lutheran high school, and his thinking is Judaic to the core: that is, moralistic, monistic, and messianic. In this it resembles Islam, the other great Semitic religion outside of Christianity. To Marxists there is one interpretation of history, and Marx is its prophet. To the Marxist, the Promised Land—that is, the socialist society which Marxists believe will arise in the future—will appear through the smoke, flame, and thunder of a glorious revolution.

China's aspirations are expressed today in communist as well as Chinese terms. Though previously known to educated Chinese as one of a number of Western systems of thought, communist ideas interested Chinese leaders when they observed the success of the Russian Revolution of 1917. Marxist-Leninist analysis was applied to the military and political problems of the Kuomintang after 1923 by Russian specialists who were invited by Sun Yat-sen to assist China. Marxist ideas were later reworked by the Chinese Communists, given an agrarian class base, and applied by Mao Tse-tung to land reform and to the remolding of Chinese society in an ingenious way. Chinese life was organized on a principle of "democratic centralism" designed to broaden involvement, elicit consent, and apply party leadership. The position of women was elevated, but the claims of the family, which had been so strong in traditional China, were subordinated to the claims of larger social units. Private enterprise in farming, business, or industry

9

came under the party or the state. The People's Liberation Army was placed under civilian, party control. Education was redesigned to promote mass literacy, technological improvement, and political adherence to Marxism-Leninism-Maoism. Literature, theater, the arts, all serve a political purpose, the creation of a strong, modern, industrialized nation with dissidence silenced.

The fact that China has accepted Marxist-Leninist leadership and rejected Christianity, even though the small remnants of the Christian church are still allowed to function in China under severe handicaps, is a deep blow to the pride of the West. In the childhood memories of many adult Americans and Europeans, there are recollections of missionaries who came to speak at the churches where they grew up, all with the same message: that China was ripe for Christianity, that with more effort, more money, the converted would come in. After the Communist victory, most missionaries were forced to leave. The bitter disillusionment and disappointment of these expectations is an important element in the underlying background of American policy. For the rural, crossroads, and small-town American a generation ago, the missionary was his window on the world. This window has now been boarded up, and a good deal of the unreasoning passion of influential American attitudes to China can be traced to the resentment which resulted. These feelings have been intensified by disappointment over the results of governmental financial aid to China since 1945 and by dismay at the methods of thought control applied by Chinese Communists to American internees and prisoners of the Korean War, and by well-financed Nationalist Chinese spokesmen and American colleagues, whose success in influencing American opinion has been the subject of public comment.

Both elements of China's history—traditional and Communist —today converge in a wave of nationalism, which seeks to transcend family and local loyalties and unify the efforts and thoughts of all Chinese. No measure of indoctrination or propaganda is neglected that can weld the country into one nation. The image of the United States as the great common enemy of the Chinese, the epitome of imperialism, and the arch-disturber of world peace has been used to further these nationalistic purposes.

We must interpret this nationalism as in large measure a deep emotional reaction to the failure of the previous society. China, the most powerful country of the world in the eighteenth century,

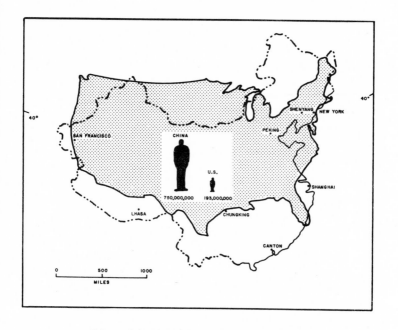

China and the United States: Area and Population

by the middle of the nineteenth century had been reduced to poverty, impotence, disorganization, and demoralization. If the impairment of our self-esteem, which the Communist success in China imposes, produces so strong an emotional reaction in us, we can hardly expect the Chinese to view their own experience at the hands of the Western countries calmly. The 100 years from 1840 to 1940 saw the continual and rapid erosion of Chinese self-esteem. It is not surprising that they have reacted by developing an intense nationalism which makes communication with them extremely difficult. Communism in China became the vehicle by which national unity was attained and an enormous clarification of national purpose achieved. China is again a power to be reckoned with. There is little doubt that very large numbers of Chinese, if not the majority, regard the present situation as a great improvement on anything they knew before 1949.

PUBLIC INFORMATION AND GOVERNMENT POLICY

Of special concern to us is the information gap among the American people about conditions inside China and even about recent events involving China's actions outside its borders. Lack of public information and concern affects American policy and obscures the issues. This ignorance is widespread, but is no longer excusable. It is difficult but entirely possible to find out a good deal about actual conditions on the Chinese mainland, and it is possible to reach some conclusions with confidence.

For example, the People's Republic now trades with more than 100 countries but has almost no trade with the United States. The People's Republic exports rice to many countries, and imports wheat. It was importing wheat from Canada and Australia because of severe shortages in China two years ago; it continues to import wheat because it earns more foreign exchange on the rice it sells than it pays out for the wheat it purchases—it makes a profit on the transactions. Furthermore, the People's Republic has so far been paying its bills on time, in Western currencies, in all its non-Asian trade.

Between 1959 and 1962 China suffered acute food shortages, along with various other shortages and maladjustments of its economy. Two kinds of factors account for the food shortages.

One was natural: severe drought and flood, which drastically reduced the agricultural output. The other kind was man-made, and fell into two categories: (1) planning error, such as the decision to concentrate too much on investment in heavy industry, and (2) political or social error, such as the decision rapidly to adopt the commune as the basic agricultural production unit. These were compounded by the sudden withdrawal of Russian technicians, who left taking their blueprints with them. Hundreds of projects were left in an incomplete and useless state representing an immense economic waste. These planning and social errors can be attributed to Communist ideology, but as was shown by the subsequent Chinese government decisions to reduce the size and alter the organization of the communes, and decrease the concentration on heavy industry, Communist leadership can adjust to necessity. China suffered from severe shortages because of ill-conceived policies and inadequate administrative structures, confronted with natural disasters and the withdrawal of Russian advisers. But there was no widespread starvation in China. The government was able to distribute food from areas of oversupply to areas of shortage. No government of China before had ever had sufficient organization and control to equalize food supplies throughout the country. The history of China since it was "opened" to the Western powers is a history of poverty, chaos, and disturbance caused in part by the crumbling of Chinese governmental effectiveness and in part by mounting population pressure. During the 100 years prior to 1949 human misery and mass starvation were unfortunately common in China. The Communist government of the People's Republic has succeeded in altering these conditions, and more Chinese are now living under decent conditions than during the previous century This fact tends to be overlooked in Western assessments which emphasize instead the dimensions of ruthlessness and totalitarianism that seem so tragic in contrast to democratic practices.

The Chinese People's Republic is clearly a well-established regime in firm control of the mainland, and it is not likely to be displaced soon. At the same time it is clear that communism is not simply and unchangeably monolithic. Relations between Russia and China are politically and ideologically completely different from those perceived before 1960. It has also become clear that the plans of the Nationalist government for reconquest of the mainland are not realistic, and that the United States is not disposed to support these efforts with armed force.

The withdrawal of Russian advisers in 1960 from the mainland, the exacerbation of the Sino-Soviet dispute, and the disappointments of the "Great Leap Forward" have placed Communist China in a position where it has been denied credits, developmental assistance, and advice essential to its plans for industrialization and modernization. Mainland China has begun to look to Western countries, and to Japan, instead of to Russia for its needs. Japan has developed its economy to an impressive extent since 1949 and could supply many of China's wants. It is interested in improving Sino-Japanese relations in return for political concessions and trade, but is held back by U.S. policy. These changes and new developments underscore the need for corresponding changes in U.S. policy to meet new opportunities. The more open situation today among the Communist countries of Central Europe is proof that change for the better can occur in the Communist world as well as in ours.

The People's Republic is engaged to the utmost of its ability in dynamic modernization and industrialization. In this process, the government seems to have the assent of the great majority of its citizens; its people are ruled not simply by force and terror. Group pressures and indoctrination are basically important, but the people of China have become eager to realize the promise of a future more attractive to them than that offered by any other regime in their recollection. Doubtless they feel the genuine excitement of personal commitment to economic development. Their government tells them that unemployment is a feature of decadent capitalism; and their socialist government puts them to work constructively; they can see and even share in the increase in production. If they have recaptured a vision of China's greatness and are proud of their country once again, it is not without cause.

None of this is to deny that the People's Republic of China is a totalitarian government, for it is; nor to deny that it employs terror as well as persuasion, for it does; nor that it is likely to achieve the development it promises without further calamities and distresses—in fact, the long-run stability of the system of economic organization now used is open to question. It is to say, however, that Chinese in many walks of life may reasonably judge that they have traded poverty for the beginnings of economic improvement, and social and political insecurity for security. How could they judge their situation as we would judge it: more regulated and controlled, less secure, and more fearful than ours? The Chinese compare the Communist present with their own past, not with our present, and their opinions are shaped by their reality, not ours.

The Plight of American Leadership

These facts about conditions in China can be validated. There is no mystery about them. They are well known. But few congressmen and American leaders are prepared to state them publicly and to act on them. There is often a lag between discarding false opinions and acting on better information. The politician waits until it is safe to change; the statesman speaks so that change becomes possible.

Since 1950 the United States and China have indulged in diatribes against each other's economic and political systems as well as denunciations of their respective policies toward each other and the world. This is a sterile and dangerous exercise. We should cease to preach to each other and proceed to a rational consideration of common problems. If this is to become possible, each side must recognize the danger that it may be trapped by its own ideology and by its assumptions about the nature of the other. Moreover, as Americans we must not demand change in China for *our* good. We must welcome change and development in China which enhances the legitimate aspirations of the Chinese.

Despite the informed dedication of many U.S. officials, governmental policy has tended to become the prisoner of public ignorance and prejudice. Our first policy changes ought to be devised to assure that our public information about China will be greatly increased, so that subsequent policy changes can be based on the public understanding that has been lacking for many years. To accomplish this requires that there be courageous leadership.

2. A FRESH LOOK AT BASIC ASSUMPTIONS

Those who call for courage in their leaders must do so with an awareness of their own responsibilities. As Americans we want our policymakers to take a courageous stand, but before we make suggestions let us look at the basic assumptions which we hope those in policymaking positions will be willing to share. We hope also to encourage public and private discussion of these basic issues on which we give our own perspectives. Our assumptions are these:

We assume the essential unity of mankind. The world is now in a time of troubles. Provincial and universal concepts of human society are in conflict. A world family of nations is struggling to be born. Just as no man is an island, so no nation or region of the earth stands alone. The human community, always a spiritual fact, has become a geographic fact, and now must become a political fact.

The anarchy of our nation-state system impedes the application of ethical principles to the international policy area. But the attempt to apply moral principles in nation-to-nation relations requires that men first give humanity itself top priority in their scale of values. This concept of the supreme value of human life has been violated through the centuries. The world has now arrived at a time when, if civilization is to be preserved, respect for human life must be given precedence in determining national policy. This means that the institutions of world community must be built so that a world without war can be a reality.

We assume the moral capacity of the Chinese. The trend toward dehumanization in our time increases as the potential of massive destruction becomes commonplace and accepted. It is easy to point out and condemn the dehumanizing elements in the adversary's policies and programs while being blind to the same things in ourselves. If we have eyes to see in our own national conduct the suspicion, self-righteousness, and reliance on immoral means which we ascribe to the Chinese Communists, we may be saved from hypocrisy and understand what turns other peoples against us and provides a constant supply of material for Chinese Communist propaganda to use against the United States.

Wrong conduct in foreign affairs is often justified by the slogan "politics is the art of the possible," but this usually implies too narrow a concept of what is possible. If Quaker experience has anything to offer, it is that no one can place limits on human potentiality, and none should underestimate the ability to respond in positive ways. The policy of the United States in Asia seems to assume that the Communist government of China understands only the language of force. But a corollary to the American belief in democracy is that all men are capable of responding politically in ways which are both humane and mutually advantageous. Are the Chinese of the People's Republic incapable of the response we expect of ourselves? We do not think so. No one knows the extent to which their responses might serve world peace, but we believe our country now wrongly ignores any such capacity.

We do well to recall in this connection that it was Chinese Communist Premier Chou En-lai who at the Bandung Conference in 1955 declared that the Chinese people were friendly to the American people and that the Chinese government was willing to enter into negotiations with the United States government to discuss existing disputes between the two countries.[7] The positive response to this suggestion led to over 120 ambassadorial talks which have been held during the ensuing decade at Warsaw. These have not been particularly fruitful but it is significant that neither side has wanted them to stop. Perhaps to create a favorable climate for these talks China released 11 Americans whose "prisoner-of-war" status was itself a matter of dispute.

It should be remembered that it was the Chinese who first proposed the exchange of newsmen (1956) and a nuclear-free Pacific (1958). Peking has now taken an adamant position, refusing to admit American newsmen (though now *we* are willing) and insisting that the United States withdraw from Taiwan as a condition for discussing the issues in conflict. It is possible that a

7. Edgar Snow, *The Other Side of the River* (New York, Random House, 1961), p. 89.

more encouraging response to its initial offer could have forestalled this hardening of attitudes. Following the explosion of a nuclear device by China, the People's Republic of China invited all nuclear powers to a conference for the discussion of disarmament and nuclear controls; we turned it down. Regardless of the grounds which United States officials may have had for believing that the offer itself was a propaganda device, the seriousness of the issue and the fact of the offer provided the United States with an opportunity to state the conditions under which it would agree to negotiate, and to press forward toward a more hopeful situation. This opportunity was missed.

We assume the consistency of ends and means. Perhaps faith is relevant to foreign policy if it is defined as the practice of right conduct in the expectation that good results will eventually follow even though immediate success or effectiveness is not assured. An application of these ideas to our China policy would mean that we would, for instance, desire and encourage the welfare of the Chinese people, while disapproving of the totalitarian and violent aspects of the People's Republic.

Though it is not a simple or an easy matter to overcome evil with good, it is even harder to overcome evil with evil. Reliance upon the threat or use of nuclear arms places the great nations (ourselves included) in the position of using evil means in an effort to do good—balancing the relative values of bomb tests which cause death and injury to the innocent and the unidentified, assessing the kind and the amount of spying and "news management" consistent with the maintenance of effective nuclear protection of our way of life, and deciding which governments may be saved and which overthrown.

To employ power in this way is to deny that there is power in doing things because they are right, and trusting that the outcome in the long run will work for good. The security of one nation cannot be achieved apart from the security and welfare of all. Half the world cannot provide adequate defense for itself by threatening the other half.

We assume that it is right to cooperate with the positive forces of social change. Despite huge expenditures on economic aid, United States foreign policy today has not sufficiently seized the opportunity to support the worldwide aspirations of the poor and the subjugated, and in these terms to challenge Communist success and power. United States preoccupation with military efforts to contain communism has caused us to forget our country's own revolutionary beginnings. We have lost sight of the demand and need for revolutionary changes in the emergent nations. These demands for changing the conditions of life for more than a billion people are multiple and complex: former colonies or minority nationalities demanding sovereign equality; the poor demanding an opportunity to raise the level of their lives; whole nations demanding speedy industrialization to catch up with the rich and powerful; and people everywhere demanding freedom and political power now that they have seen that it is possible for them to attain it.

A foreign policy supporting this revolution of rising expectations must rely far less upon military power and far more on technical assistance and the kind of foreign aid which helps people help themselves. If considerations of expediency in waging ideological war cancel out considerations of justice and prudence in waging war against illiteracy, poverty, and disease, even the best efforts are wasted. Sensitivity to human needs can release the highest values in our American heritage and provide a far greater challenge to those powers we oppose, both within our own lives and in the world, than maintaining an arsenal capable of destroying all humanity. Instead of vast sums appropriated for military purposes, we advocate projects which like the Peace Corps attack evils at their roots and create the conditions which alone can remove the occasion for war.

We assume that improvement is possible. We are not strangers to the discouragment that flows from the complexity and the frustrations of attempting to build a better world, but we are convinced that to surrender to discouragement is folly. We are encouraged by the increasing number of Americans who believe that our security is identified with the security of all mankind. U.S. policy has moved from nearly exclusive reliance upon nuclear deterrence to the test ban treaty, to détente with the Soviet Union, to the hot line agreement, to the Arms Control and Disarmament Agency, to the Peace Corps, and to renewed negotiations for disarmament. These are among the hopeful achievements of our time, and they are proof that concrete change for peace and a better world is a practical reality and a continuing possibility.

We are encouraged to propose policies which we believe can

lead to similarly improved relations with the People's Republic of China. We are aware that there will continue to be profound differences in ideology and practice, but even such an elementary step as American acceptance of the fact of the Chinese revolution would itself reduce the intensity of the hostility between the United States and China and provide an opening for further hopeful change.

We assume the importance of maintaining a capacity for flexibility. New situations provide new opportunities. Many of our allies have taken a different course from the one the United States has pursued. Great Britain recognizes China and carries on commercial relations. Australia and Canada sell China large amounts of wheat. In 1964 France extended diplomatic recognition, a move which the French feel could increase diplomatic freedom of maneuver and pave the way for a general settlement.

The times are favorable to change. Relations with the U.S.S.R. increasingly depend upon objective factors rather than the whim of the head of the government. France aspires to a greater role in Asian affairs. And now, fatefully, China has achieved nuclear capability, a fact which adds urgency to efforts for general and complete disarmament. China's policy toward the United States has been as fruitless as U.S. policy has been. Chinese hostility toward the United States has been fanned for purposes of domestic control. But it is possible that China's desire for technological development, for more rapid modernization, and for an accepted place in the family of nations would produce a more friendly response if American policy should change. We believe that the time is ripe for American initiatives based on this assumption.

3. NEW POLICY TOWARD CHINA

In a speech before the United States Senate on March 25, 1964, Senator J. William Fulbright said: "As we have seen in our relations with Germany and Japan, hostility can give way in an astonishingly short time to close friendship; and, as we have seen in our relations with China, the reverse can occur with equal speed. It is not impossible that in our time our relations with China will change again—if not in friendship, then perhaps to 'competitive coexistence.' It would therefore be extremely useful if we could introduce an element of flexibility, or more precisely of the capacity to be flexible, into our relations with Communist China."[8]

The call for a more flexible China policy here expressed by Senator Fulbright is being voiced by an increasing number of Americans. We join in this call.

FIRST STEPS

Where solutions to problems depend upon mutual agreement, it is often a temptation for one side or the other to accommodate to a situation of "no solution," blaming the obduracy of the other side. This is especially true when the differences are complex, when the issues seem to be rooted in conflict over fundamental principle, and where present decisions may affect future status. When one side or the other adopts an attitude of blaming the other side, the practical effect is to encourage a similar response. The result is that stubbornness on one side reinforces self-righteousness on the other.

A more creative approach can often be opened up by either side, even in the absence of agreement, if it wants to produce a change for the better and is willing to explore initiatives which may be undertaken unilaterally as a prelude to multilateral negotiation and eventual agreement. The resolution of conflict and

8. U.S. Congress, *Congressional Record, Proceedings and Debates,* 88th Cong., 2nd Sess. (1964), Vol. 110, No. 56.

the achievement of right relationships often depend upon such a desire and willingness. Much depends upon one side or the other having the strength, the confidence, and the imagination to undertake initiatives arising out of right principle and goodwill, and to appeal to the goodwill and the right principles of the other side. This is possible only if it is not assumed that the truth is all on one side and the evil all on the other. If we remain open to the possibility of imperfection on our own side, and assume that there is at least some capacity for good on the other, we can then speak with nonjudgmental candor and in hopeful expectation of an eventual positive response. Initiatives taken in this spirit can carry a dispute out of a deadlock and into creative resolution.

In the case of China and the relationships of the United States to Asia, this kind of approach could stimulate initiatives that could be taken by the United States without requiring at the start the agreement of the Chinese and without endangering the legitimate interests of the United States or of those to whose security and interests we feel ourselves committed. Among such initiatives are the following:

1. *We could move to halt the military threats and incursions against the mainland by Taiwan.*

Since 1950 and before, U.S. relations with the People's Republic of China have been hostile: espionage has been admitted; the American delegation at the United Nations has organized and led the opposition to the admission of Communist China; the U.S. has embargoed trade with China under the Trading with the Enemy Act, and has sought agreement of other nations to do the same. The Republic of China on Taiwan has publicly reported its hostile acts, in order to give some sense of reality to its expressed intent of counterrevolution and return. These have included harassment of shipping, attempts to blockade certain ports, reconnaissance overflights, bombing, shelling, and commando raids on the coast, occasional actions by armed bands, sabotage, espionage, and dropping propaganda leaflets. Despite occasional U.S. disclaimers of responsibility, many of these actions could not have been carried out without U.S. funds or equipment and its tacit approval as well. It is not necessary to detail the times and places and effect of all of these moves—some of them sporadic, some continuous—in order to understand that there has been a more or less continuous military struggle. One of the situations supporting the sporadic attacks on the mainland is the Nationalist occupation and massive fortification of the small offshore islands of Quemoy and Matsu. The garrisoning of more than one-third of the total Nationalist troops on these islands is more of a threat to the mainland than a protection for Taiwan. The use of these islands as bases for attacks on Communist shipping or for raids on the mainland is not consistent with Nationalist or American security. Quemoy, the major such base, is only four miles from the mainland and lies in the approaches of the harbor of Amoy, a major mainland port. The Nationalist position there, with heavy American military support, remains a standing affront to the Communist government and a chronic source of dangerous tension. These offshore islands are clearly not part of Taiwan. Both for the better security of Taiwan and in order to create a more favorable climate for negotiation, Nationalist occupation should be withdrawn from the offshore islands. If necessary the United States could exert pressure by declining to provide the necessary military support for the maintenance of the bases there and by offering to support the withdrawal. The relatively small local population, fishermen and farmers, should be offered completely free choice of remaining or moving to Taiwan as part of the Nationalist withdrawal.

U.S. refusal to recognize the People's Republic of China and U.S. support of Chiang Kai-shek have been expressions of hostility described as undeclared war or near-war. Chiang Kai-shek has pledged again and again his support for sabotage and uprisings on the mainland and is committed, at least officially, to recover control of China. In 1958 the then Secretary of State Dulles could argue, "The United States holds the view that Communism's rule in China is not permanent and that one day it will pass. By withholding recognition from Peiping it seeks to hasten that passing."[9]

This near-war against the People's Republic of China can no longer be justified on the ground of the "passing" nature of that government. It is the strongest regime China has known in modern times and it is growing stronger. U.S. support of the Republic of China's attempts at counterrevolution has borne only the bitter fruit of mutual fear and hatred. We are increasingly alone in our hostility, as even our allies (to say nothing of the neutrals and the

9. U.S. Dept. of State *Bulletin, 39,* No. 1002 (September 8, 1958).

nonaligned) drop away, believing it is wrong to refuse to deal with China on any level. Even India, although regarding itself as a victim of Communist Chinese aggression, still advocates the acknowledgment in the United Nations that the People's Republic of China is the rightful occupant of China's seat in the Security Council and the General Assembly. For the United States to take the initiative in calling a halt to warlike attitudes and warlike measures against China would jeopardize no valid interest and would open the way for other constructive steps.

2. *We could acknowledge that the People's Republic of China is the government of China.*

To recognize the People's Republic of China is a diplomatic act which looks toward reciprocation and an exchange of ambassadors. But the acknowledgment by the United States that the People's Republic of China is in fact the government of China is only a matter of stating the obvious, and is something our government could do on its own initiative. The illusory nature of American policy toward China is suggested by the consistency with which the United States since 1950 has based its policy in Asia on the proposition that the government of China is located in Taiwan.

The decision not to accord diplomatic recognition to the People's Republic of China was based in part on the belief that failure to extend recognition would somehow inhibit the success of the new regime. Actually the reverse has proved to be the case. Our attempt to exclude China from the world community has relieved it of the responsibilities of United Nations participation, it has deepened U.S. ignorance of China's internal development, and it has allowed China's nuclear weapons capacity to emerge unchallenged and unfettered by international obligations, the burden of which it has not had to assume, thanks largely to the United States. It has meant that the United States has become a convenient hate symbol in a period of dynamic Chinese growth and development. It has impaired the capacity of the United Nations to deal effectively with problems affecting world peace and involving the government of almost a fourth of the population of the earth.

No one can say what the immediate response of China would be to the acknowledgment by the United States of the sovereignty of the People's Republic, but this is an essential step which the U.S. can and must take if a base is to be laid for relationships less dangerous and potentially more effective than the present mutual isolation.

3. *We could demonstrate our concern for the well-being of China.*

Whatever the differences may be between the United States and China, they must not be allowed to assume the proportions of a war against or indifference toward the Chinese people. This is not said with any desire to separate the people of China from their government, but rather to remind ourselves of the limits which men of goodwill must impose upon themselves and their governments when international tensions become chronic. In the same way that individuals must show respect for each other before there can be genuine friendship, so nations must deal with each other in terms that acknowledge mutual dignity and respect. The differences between overweening nationalism and justifiable national dignity are matters of degree rather than of principle. We do not know whether China would stop its virulent attacks on the intentions and the good faith of the United States if the U.S. accorded China the normal courtesies of international relations, but we do know that China is not likely to change if we do not.

Basic to China's present development is the commitment to raise the level of life of the Chinese people. It is pressing hard to increase food production, develop and direct the use of national resources for broad public purposes, improve the level of educational and health resources, build industry, and move forward into the front rank of the technologically developed nations. Success will mean vastly improved conditions of life for the Chinese people—and, if the Soviet Union's experience is relevant, a relaxation of harsh measures of control over the minds as well as the labor of the people. Improved education inevitably promises greater freedom. It is in the interests of the people of China and also in our own interests that these efforts succeed. To be willing to support them through trade and technical assistance is consistent both with human brotherhood and with our long-term national interest. We need not approve the totalitarian government of China any more than we approve many of the unfree governments now sharing membership in the United Nations, but we should desire the welfare of the Chinese and share their sorrow when disaster or hardship befalls them. As Americans we are concerned by the restrictions on individual freedom which the Chinese revolution has imposed, and annoyed by Chinese accusations and self-righteousness toward the U.S. However, let us not give way to anger, for we should remind ourselves that we may often give a similar impression of self-righteousness. Moreover, the U.S. is freer to explore the requirements of a growing world community than is a China involved in the all-consuming fervor of a new nationalism. Out of our awareness of the interdependence of all, we should make it clear that we are concerned for Chinese welfare, both because it is right to be concerned and because we know that our own welfare and theirs are interdependent.

4. *We could end American restrictions on communication and exchange with the People's Republic of China.*

A group of American newsmen authorized by our government to travel in China has been refused entry for many months, but for most of the years since 1949 the restrictions against travel either way have been imposed also by our country. Our government and mass media have become attached to the term "bamboo curtain" because of its neat parallel to Churchill's "Iron Curtain" and because it suggests that the blame for the absence of communication is China's. But the truth is that we have done our share in raising the barriers. Because we need to understand China at first hand, and because it is wrong to isolate Americans and Chinese from each other, we propose that our government should announce the end of its special restrictions on travel between the two countries. This does not mean that equitable controls on travel, sojourn, and immigration would not apply, but simply that our relations in these respects would be as they are with other countries. The need for communication is urgent. When the People's Republic reciprocates, the U.S. should actively aid in plans for visits and exchanges of newsmen, scholars, teachers, students, businessmen and their counterparts among China's managerial group, labor union members, professionals, farmers, government employees, representatives of art and culture, and tourists. The People's Republic has proved it is not a "passing phase"; we should take the initiative against the mutual ignorance and misinformation between our countries.

These exchanges would have to be undertaken through the various government-sponsored cultural associations which take the place in the People's Republic of our private voluntary organizations. Though this is not ideal in terms of people-to-people exchange, it would be a step in the right direction, as experience with the U.S.S.R. has demonstrated. Other forms of communication, including books and periodicals, motion pictures, and television and radio programs should be exchanged freely. A wealth of mutual enrichment can also come from cultural exchange in music, drama, and the visual arts; beauty is a binding and universal force.

American public ignorance of contemporary China and Chinese ignorance of us are among the chief reasons for the tension and hostility between us. This is dangerous in itself, and it threatens the peace of the world. If both sides can be freer to learn more about each other, tension and hostility seem certain to decrease. The present Chinese image of the U.S. feeds Chinese hostility, but it is a warped and perverted image which we should be eager to correct. Fuller knowledge on both sides will make better relations possible, and without it the chances of any improvement are poor. Broad and varied communication between the two peoples is essential.

5. *We could end our special restrictions on trade with China.*

We could treat trade with China as we treat trade with the Soviet Union. If this were done, there is no assurance that there would be any immediate response from the People's Republic. They have said that they are willing to trade with everyone except the U.S. In the light of the eagerness of Japan and our European allies to trade with China, the Chinese might at first consider any advantage in trading with the U.S. as insufficient to outweigh our value to them as Enemy Number One.

Possibly the most that could happen at first would be a beginning of a three-cornered trade in which we would buy from Hong Kong and other Asian countries goods which had originated in China, and would sell in the same Asian markets goods which were then transshipped to China. It is questionable whether the quantity of such goods would be significant commercially at least in the initial stages. What would be significant is that our government would no longer be putting our own importers and exporters at a disadvantage, and our trade policy would no longer give evidence of a hostile attitude toward China.

6. *We could declare our readiness to join China in projects of mutual advantage and concern.*

Although the immediate prospect for large-scale exchanges remains dim, there are steps which the United States could conceivably take, either by itself or in cooperation with the Chinese, to encourage the pooling of knowledge and resources. A good example is language teaching. It would be to the advantage of both parties if more Chinese had a knowledge of English and if more Americans could speak Chinese. Important advances have been made in the teaching of languages. There would be value in bringing linguistic experts together to discuss means of improving basic communication through the learning of these two very different languages.

A second major area of concern is that of world population growth and the resultant pressures and demands upon world resources. No other problem is as crucial to China's efforts to raise the economic level of its people. Tremendous progress has been made in the United States in recent years in developing birth spacing and control techniques. China has also experimented with various approaches to the population problem. Both have engaged in research and exchange of information with experts of other countries, but the political impasse prohibits direct contact between the specialists of these two countries. There are significant findings for them to exchange in the hope that children in both countries may be born to a full life where health, knowledge, and a chance to develop their capacities can be provided. It is in the interest of both the Chinese government and the American government to have all the information available from whatever source. Each would benefit from sharing knowledge on birth control methods, and political antagonisms should not be a barrier to mutually advantageous exchange.

A third group of services of mutual benefit would be the sharing of information and techniques in various scientific and technical areas such as water resources and control, irrigation, erosion, soil fertilization, and plant genetics. Chinese and American experts in such fields should welcome an opportunity to exchange their knowledge in a completely nonpolitical way which would nevertheless contribute both to economic development and to the improvement of relations between our two peoples. For example, a newly established International Rice Research Institute at Los Banos in the Philippines is developing a quick-maturing, short-stalk rice plant which will not easily flatten during windstorms. The results of its work would be useful to China.

7. *We could prepare for negotiations with the People's Republic of China on mutual problems.*

Still another area in which the United States can act is in planning for discussions and negotiations with the Chinese. A decision to acknowledge and to recognize the People's Republic of China requires a new analysis of all our relationships in Asia and the Pacific. Both nations must negotiate bilateral and multilateral agreements dealing with shared opportunities and problems including, most urgently, agreements to ban nuclear testing. China invited negotiation on disarmament immediately after it exploded its first nuclear device. Few Americans realize that the United States did in fact negotiate with China in 1962, when we became cosignatories with the People's Republic of China to the treaty guaranteeing the neutrality and independence of Laos. We should communicate to the People's Republic of China our willingness to negotiate directly and with the other nations involved on all issues now in dispute between us. We believe that the American people would respond favorably to such leadership.[10] Only if we are ready to discuss problems can we expect the People's Republic to join the community of nations and to be subject, as we are, to developing world opinion, conscience, and precedent which, through the United Nations and through other facilities and agencies, is in effect the emerging fabric of world law.

Each of the policies proposed in this chapter could be carried out without prior agreement or immediate response from the People's Republic of China, but this would not invalidate the

10. In a 1964 survey the response to the question: "Suppose the President suggested that we talk over problems of Asia with Communist China and try to come to some agreements with them?" was 71 per cent in favor, 19 per cent against. "The American Public's View of U.S. Policy Toward China," a report prepared for the Council on Foreign Relations by the Survey Research Center, University of Michigan, p. 29.

new direction. Above all, such a new policy direction, even though unilaterally undertaken, would end the ironical and dangerous situation which obtains at the time of this writing when U.S. conduct to a great extent conforms to the Chinese Communist doctrinaire view of us.

Whatever the outcome of any unilateral acts from the American side, some attempt to break the present deadlock is long and dangerously overdue. Two of the largest and most powerful nations of the world have since 1950 lived largely in isolated ignorance of one another and in an atmosphere of mutual fear and hate. Even if we must act alone in taking the first steps toward a more rational relationship, the present situation is dangerously alienated from reality and must not be allowed to continue. Under any circumstances, we can assume that a change of any sort in U.S. policy will produce a changed response from China. This is the nature of relations between nations. Changes in American policy are a necessary prelude to bringing about the kinds of changes Americans would like to see in Chinese policy. Clearly specified and carefully explained actions that express goodwill can proceed in the faith that they will ultimately evoke a like response.

4. COMMUNICATING WITH COMMUNIST CHINA THROUGH THE UNITED NATIONS

CHINA AS A GREAT POWER IN THE UNITED NATIONS

The basic assumption of this report is that it is necessary and possible to break through the barriers to communication which separate the government and people of the United States from the government and people of China. We believe also that it is both right and in the interest of the United States to encourage as much interaction as possible between China and the other nations of the world. If China is to support the peace of the world, it must first become more intimately and widely involved with the world as a whole. If interaction is to take place, the People's Republic must take China's seat in the U.N., the major center for international communication. In the U.N., representatives of member states engage in both formal and informal discussion of a broad agenda of international problems, political, economic, social and cultural. Since the U.N. headquarters are in the United States, interaction with China within the U.N. context would presumably have particular impact on the American image of China and on the Chinese image of the United States.

Some have argued that the People's Republic of China is not a "peace-loving nation" and would be so disruptive an influence in the U.N. that it should be barred from membership. Others argue that the People's Republic would be influenced toward more cooperative behavior if it is within this international organization rather than outside it. Both arguments are based on too simple a view of reality. China, as one of the "big five" in the U.N. system, would become involved in a wide range of relationships, some potentially tension-creating and some potentially tension-reducing.

As a major power, China would be expected to send to New York, Geneva, and other sites of U.N.-related activity skilled diplomats instructed to work energetically for China's vital interests. Since China would participate in almost every aspect of the United Nations system—not only the committees of the General Assembly and Security Council and the policymaking bodies of the Specialized Agencies but also in the many working subcommittees and the political caucuses—its membership would have a major impact on the whole pattern of relationships among U.N. member states. This continuing process of participation would, whatever the immediate strains, encourage a sense of international responsibility on China's part.

Within the U.N. China would confront three major diplomatic forces: as a member of the Soviet caucus China would be in constant negotiation with other Communist countries in their attempt to present a united front on major issues at the U.N.; as a leading member of the Afro-Asian caucus China would have constant contact with the developing countries; as a member of the Security Council and as a member of most other important U.N. organs China would constantly face the representatives of the United States and other Western governments and of the world press.

The Soviet caucus, a unified voting bloc at the U.N. heretofore dominated by the U.S.S.R., would initially come under joint Sino-Soviet leadership. There would be constant negotiation behind the scenes and possibly some healing of the Sino-Soviet rift. Alternatively, a failure of bloc unity could lead to open rivalry in the U.N. between these two Communist "great powers." Of all forms of interaction within the U.N. system, this could be the most intense and the most problematical. Should bloc unity be preserved, some of the East European states might find themselves playing a mediatory role, gaining more freedom of action on specific issues but submitting to the ideological restraints of Communist solidarity.

The People's Republic of China would almost certainly be included in the Afro-Asian consultative caucus, although Nationalist China has not been. How long this large and diverse group of nations could cooperate at the U.N. in the face of this new power relationship is problematical. The increased number of African nations, no longer so dependent on Asian support at the U.N., might conceivably seek to preserve their nonalignment by relying on an exclusively African caucus rather than associating their efforts with China. If, however, the Afro-Asian group continues, Peking would probably use the contacts it provides to project an image of China as a leader of the developing countries. Within this caucus the Chinese would have to vie for leadership with India and with the United Arab Republic.

Dialogue at the U.N. between the U.S.A. and China could take place on two levels: public debate and quiet negotiation. In public debate the People's Republic might well be a more bitter opponent than the U.S.S.R. The clash of interests between the U.S.A. and China at the U.N. would be especially sharp on the issues on Taiwan, Korea, and Indochina. China doubtless would have the support of the Soviet bloc, but probably could not get majority support. On the political issues that are brought before the Security Council China would of course have a veto, which, if used on resolutions acceptable to the U.S.S.R., would further check the Council's ability to act.

The United States at present maintains at Warsaw the sole communication link for off-the-record discussion with the Chinese. There would be the possibility of further links at the U.N., both through contacts between the permanent missions of the two countries and through possible off-the-record discussions with the Secretary-General. The willingness of the two countries to use informal channels available through the U.N. may not develop during the initial period of confrontation, but could be of immense value in the event of any crisis.

Chinese diplomats living in New York City would be first-hand observers of the American scene, reporting their impressions to Peking. These same diplomats, both in their public presentations and in their very presence in the U.S.A., would be the subject of much comment by U.S. newspapers. While press reactions can be valuable in establishing a framework of reality, they have often created a dangerous sense of conflict and crisis which otherwise might not have arisen.

SPECIFIC WORKING RELATIONSHIPS

As an adherent to the U.N. Charter and ipso facto to the Statute of the International Court, the People's Republic of China,

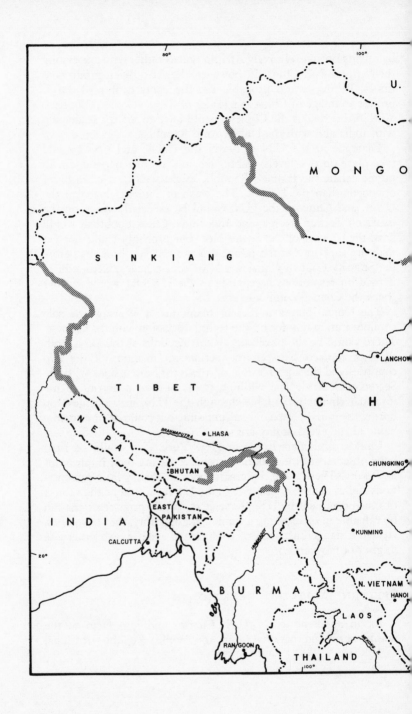

CHINA AND EAST ASIA

if seated, would be obligated to a whole series of legal commitments. As a member of the Sixth (Legal) Committee of the General Assembly, it would take part in the deliberations on "Principles of International Law Concerning Friendly Relations and Cooperation Among States." There is no way of knowing whether it would consider itself bound by Nationalist China's acceptance of compulsory jurisdiction provisions of the Court (1946) or alternatively would insist on a self-judging reservation similar to that embodied in the U.S.A.'s Connally amendment. It probably would insist, as other Communist countries have, that no doctrine or convention of international law is valid unless expressly accepted by the individual state.

As a major military power and as one of the five members of the so-called nuclear club, China could participate in disarmament negotiations regardless of its status in the U.N. The existing 18-Nation Disarmament Committee at Geneva, the proposed nuclear summit conference, and the all-inclusive disarmament commission proposed by the Cairo Conference of September 1964 would all be technically separate from the U.N. However, China's role in the General Assembly would permit it to take part in the U.N.'s annual discussion and review of disarmament, with opportunities to put before the 115 member nations the Chinese point of view. The People's Republic would be interested in neutralizing U.S. nuclear superiority in the Pacific and would doubtless introduce its proposals for banning the use of nuclear weapons and for the creation of a nuclear-free zone in the Pacific.

Of continuing concern in the United Nations is its peacekeeping capabilities. Can the experience of U.N. "presences" of varying types in crisis situations be brought to bear on the development of a system of peacekeeping operations which will have the support of all major powers? The U.N. could hardly attempt to establish any type of presence in any East or Southeast Asian crisis area without consultation with the Peking government. Until this question is explored with the Chinese, the U.N.'s capability for peacekeeping in Asia remains clouded. The possibility should not be excluded that the Peking government might have a vital interest in stability which would permit use of the U.N.

The effects of the participation of the People's Republic in the economic policies and projects of the U.N. are not easy to predict. China, like India, has vast human needs. Both countries are

SOME OF THE U.N. BODIES IN WHICH THE CHINESE PEOPLE'S REPUBLIC MIGHT SIT AS A U.N. MEMBER

Security Council

Military Staff Committee (inactive)

General Assembly and its 7 committees of the whole (Political, Special Political, Economic, Social, Dependent Territories, Administrative and Budgetary, Legal)

General (steering) Committee

Peace Observation Committee (largely inactive)

Committee on Government Replies on the Question of Defining Aggression

Subsidiary Bodies

Trusteeship Council (becoming inactive)

Economic Commission for Asia and the Far East

Statistical Commission

Population Commission

Technical Assistance Committee

Social Commission

Commission on Narcotic Drugs

Executive Board of UNICEF

Executive Committee of the High Commissioner's Program (for refugees)

Economic and Social Council*

Specialized Agencies

International Atomic Energy Agency

International Labor Organization

U.N. Educational, Scientific and Cultural Organization

World Health Organization

International Bank

International Monetary Fund

International Development Association

International Civil Aviation Organization

Universal Postal Union

International Telecommunication Union

World Meteorological Organization

Inter-Governmental Maritime Consultative Organization

U.N. Trade and Development Board (proposed)*

Food and Agriculture Organization*

*Membership seats not now held by Nationalist China but open to Chinese representation in the future.

struggling against poverty and are seeking rapid industrialization; both have excellent intellectual resources, but both lack specific scientific techniques and experience which are available only from Japan, the U.S.S.R., and the Western industrial countries. Yet here the similarity ends, because India permits the maximum use of U.N. technical assistance and capital-financing institutions. By contrast, the Chinese practice could be similar to that of other Communist nations: hesitation to guarantee the rights of access and freedom of movement required by the U.N. in all host countries.[11] China might be more interested in providing than in receiving internationally sponsored technical assistance.

The agencies and commissions of the U.N. system which require the participation of officials who operate in areas other than those of political diplomacy promote communication of knowledge and techniques beneficial to all nations. China would have an interest in participating in international conferences in such fields, among others, as scientific agriculture, conservation of water resources, peaceful uses of atomic energy, control of epidemic diseases, promotion of safety in air and sea travel, and weather control and telecommunication. Under U.N. fellowship programs, China could both send and receive students in specialized fields of knowledge. In each instance China, like all other U.N. members, would have the right to decide which U.N. personnel were acceptable and which opportunities for overseas experience it considered appropriate. Though factors of pride and suspicion can limit the use of the opportunities provided by the U.N. system, over a period of time such barriers tend to become less obstructive.

Furthermore, in the policymaking bodies of all these agencies and commissions the Chinese, insofar as they accepted participation, would need to expound and seek support for their positions. This very process involves knowing the positions of other nations

11. Within recent years there has been a small but increasing number of U.N. missions in some Communist nations: Mongolia, Romania, Poland, and Albania. It may be relevant to note at this point that the greater the degree to which a country is free from U.S.S.R. political domination, the more willing it is to utilize U.N. technical assistance. The outstanding example is Yugoslavia, which has been an enthusiastic recipient under many U.N.-sponsored programs.

and estimating voting trends within the various international organizations. The involvement of officials from many specialized fields in this process would tend to discourage the focusing of hostility and would tend to diversify and to multiply modes of communication.

The Economic Commission for Asia and the Far East (ECAFE) is one of the international organizations in which the People's Republic of China could cooperate on practical programs with a minimum of ideological conflict. This consultative organization includes all the nations of Asia and seven non-Asian industrial nations with economic interests in Asia (including the U.S.A., the U.S.S.R., the United Kingdom, and France). This is the commission which has sponsored international planning for the development of the resources of the valley of the Mekong River, which flows from sources in southwestern China through Laos, Cambodia, Thailand, and South Vietnam. The Commission both conducts and coordinates research on problems of economic development and, through the newly established Asian Institute of Economic Development, helps train administrators. The establishment of a Development Bank for Asia is now being discussed in ECAFE. The participation of the People's Republic in ECAFE, like the participation of the Soviet Union in the Economic Commission for Europe, could provide a bridge of common interest across ideological gulfs.

The People's Republic would, like all other nations, have an influence on the International Civil Service. Nearly all of the 47 persons of Chinese Nationalist origin in the upper ranks of the U.N. Secretariat are at present on permanent tenure, while more than 80 per cent of the personnel of Eastern European origin are on short-term appointments. Presumably the People's Republic would nominate civil servants whose primary ties are to the nation rather than the international organization. Though this could cause some difficulty, there would be no major breakdown of U.N. efficiency because many of the jobs so filled are primarily technical in nature.

IMPACT OF CHINESE REPRESENTATION

This brief survey of the potential role of the People's Republic of China in the many councils, committees, and informal groupings of the U.N. indicates that China would be involved in experience of vital communication which could in the long run alter its view of the world and its attitude toward the United States. The People's Republic would have journalists at the U.N., and Peking could even be host to a U.N. Information Center similar to those in Moscow and Prague. Although these information sources might be strictly controlled, the Peking government, through its need to justify its policies before the U.N., would necessarily create some awareness among its own people of the significance of the U.N. in world affairs.

Perhaps the most immediate impact of the possible representation of the People's Republic of China would be its effect on U.S. public attitudes. Under its legal obligations to the U.N., the U.S.A. would be host to a major Communist Chinese diplomatic mission in New York. American diplomats would be communicating formally, and perhaps informally, with diplomats of the Peking government. The U.S. Congress might find itself asked to vote money for U.N. projects from which the Chinese derive benefit. Under these circumstances, the challenge to American diplomacy would be to develop policies which would strengthen rather than weaken governmental and popular support of the U.N. The alternative for the U.S.A. would be gradual withdrawal of political and economic investment in the U.N., with consequent losses in communication with *all* Afro-Asian nations, both Communists and non-Communist.

The seating of the representatives of the People's Republic of China would be one important element in a broader effort to break through the barriers to communication between China and the West. The long-range potentialities for Chinese cooperation in the U.N. would include the reduction of Cold War tensions in East Asia and the promotion of steps toward disarmament, world law, and international cooperation for the achievement of human dignity. No step will be easy. But the alternative is not just a continuation of the status quo in East Asia but rather mounting tension, an acceleration of the arms race, and increasing danger of war.

This report will not attempt to deal with the specific legal procedures for achieving participation of the Peking government in the United Nations. These have been dealt with extensively elsewhere.[12] Any decision is complicated by three factors:

1. The announced unwillingness of Peking to make any concessions in order to gain representation.

2. The procedural ambiguities arising from the fact that the Charter has no provisions covering the question of rival contenders for a nation's seat.

3. The desire of the Chinese Nationalists, with the strong support of the U.S.A., to preserve their U.N. status.

Whatever may be the procedural method, there is a strong likelihood that once a decision is made in the General Assembly, other U.N. bodies will follow suit.

The greatest political barrier to interaction with the People's Republic of China within the U.N. context is the existence of the Republic of China, the effective government of over two million Chinese (who fled the mainland in 1949) and ten million Taiwanese, descendants of settlers who came from China nearly 300 years ago. If the claims of the China of Chiang Kai-shek did not exist, the Peking government would probably be participating in the U.N. today. In putting emphasis on the importance of acknowledging the right of the People's Republic to China's seat in the U.N., the authors of this report realize that such a move would bring to a head the long-festering problem of the future status of Taiwan. As a result, they are particularly concerned that the American people take a fresh look at the intricacies of the problem of the 12 million people who live in Taiwan.

12. Robert P. Newman, *The Recognition of Communist China* (New York, Macmillan, 1961), p. 92.

5. TOWARD A RESOLUTION OF THE TAIWAN PROBLEM

Central to the issues that divide China and the United States is Taiwan (Formosa). The positions taken have hardened over the years, complicating both the problem of diplomatic recognition and the seating of the People's Republic in the United Nations.

In 1960 Premier Chou En-lai said: "It is inconceivable that a peace pact can be concluded without diplomatic relations between China and the United States. It is also inconceivable that there can be diplomatic relations between China and the United States without a settlement of the dispute between the two countries in the Taiwan region."[13]

On April 20, 1964, President Lyndon Johnson said, "It is not we who must reexamine our view of China, it is the Chinese Communists who must reexamine their view of the world. . . . Nor can anyone doubt our unalterable commitment to the defense and liberty of free China."[14]

The United States has made commitments to the Republic of China on Taiwan which cannot be immediately canceled. To the People's Republic, Taiwan is an integral part of China, and it believes the Taiwan problem to be a domestic one in which outside interference is considered to be an aggressive act. If the deadlock reflected in these positions is to be ended and peaceful relations are to be established between the People's Republic and the U.S., each must strive to understand and appreciate the position of the other and not merely defend its own.

THE FACTUAL BACKGROUND

Taiwan is regarded by both the Nationalists and the Communists as a province of China. It was settled, beginning on a

---

13. Snow, *The Other Side of the River*, p. 88.

14. Speech at Associated Press Luncheon, New York, April 20, 1964, quoted in *Congressional Quarterly*, April 24, 1964, p. 793.

large scale in the seventeenth century, by Chinese who came from the mainland provinces nearest to it. They dispossessed the aborigines and developed the arable land near the sea. From 1870 the island came increasingly under Japanese influence as the Chinese government grew weaker in its role of titular sovereign on the island. From 1895, at the end of the first Sino-Japanese War, until 1945 and the Allied defeat of Japan, Taiwan was an important and integral part of the Japanese empire. During these 50 years as a colony, Japanese capital and management were responsible for the island's modern economic development. They created an educational system, built most of the capital city of Taipei, and laid out an excellent network of railways, roads, and telecommunications. In particular, the agricultural system, still the dominant basis of the island's economy, was transformed into a consistent producer of surpluses and an important source of sugar for export. As one measure of the Japanese success in promoting Taiwan's economic development, its population nearly tripled. The experience as a whole had profound effects on the Taiwanese by making them feel different from mainland Chinese. Japanese control was resented, but Taiwan gained from Japanese investment and management and also became associated with Japanese culture.

At the Cairo Conference in 1943, the United States gave support to China's claim to Taiwan, joining the British in declaring that "All territories Japan had stolen from the Chinese, such as Manchuria, Formosa, and the Pescadores, shall be returned to the Republic of China." On August 30, 1945, the Chinese government declared its sovereignty over Taiwan, and on October 15 the Japanese government formally handed it back to China. In an official memorandum (April 18, 1947) U.S. Ambassador J. Leighton Stuart stated: "The Formosan Chinese greeted the surrender of Japanese authority to the Chinese with immense enthusiasm on October 15, 1945. After fifty years under Japanese control . . . they welcomed a return to China, which they had idealized as the 'Mother Country.' "[15]

The harsh political repression which followed, however, as Chiang Kai-shek's government effectively suppressed all Taiwan-

15. *United States Relations with China,* Dept. of State Publication 3573 (August 1949), p. 923.

ese attempts at expression or gestures toward representation in the new government, created widespread bitterness. When the Nationalist government, plus roughly two million mainland Chinese, fled to Taiwan in 1949–50 before the victorious Communist armies, the hostility of the Taiwanese toward the mainlanders was intensified. Bitterness over continued political repression (in which most of the would-be political leaders among the Taiwanese were assassinated or jailed) was increased by the "carpetbagging" of mainland officials and businessmen and their exploitation of the Taiwanese. Since 1945 very few Taiwanese, as distinct from mainland Chinese, have held any important political, business, educational, or other prominent or profitable positions.

Since 1949–50, when the Nationalist government of China became in effect only the government of Taiwan, massive American financial aid and technical assistance have been channeled into Taiwan. Military expenditures account for a large portion of American support, but there has been substantial economic aid as well. Partly because Taiwan is a relatively small area, the impact of the American-financed and American-directed development programs has been great. American administrative and even policymaking influence may have been as important as financial aid. The sweeping and very successful land reform program on Taiwan, for example, would almost certainly not have been carried out in anything like the form it took if it had not been for American advice and direction. The economy of Taiwan, though still dependent on American aid, has become vigorously healthy and has begun to reach the point where it might become independently viable.

There seems no question that, even with the alarmingly rapid natural growth of population in this small area, plus the influx of some two million refugees from the mainland in 1949–50, the average Taiwanese is substantially better off economically than he has ever been and that the prospects for continued improvement are good. Taiwan's economic growth since 1950 and its land reform program are in fact a genuine success story in an Asia where such successes have not been common. Although political life, especially for the Taiwanese, is still far from free, the economic success has been and remains a product of joint Sino-American effort, one in which large numbers of able and dedicated Chinese and Americans have worked together rather than merely an operation for which the United States has paid the bills.

For example, the work of the Joint Committee on Rural Reconstruction, which carried forward the land reform program and continues to direct agricultural improvement, has demonstrated that creative joint ventures can succeed if there are safeguards to protect them from political pressures. This agency's work has vitally affected the lives of Taiwanese farmers, providing opportunities for initiative, self-expression, and cooperative action in the application of new techniques, the use of new seeds and fertilizers, and the development of new forms of organization. A large number of American agencies, public and private, carry on programs of relief, economic development, education, and missionary activity on the island. American business firms have increasing dealings with Chinese in Taiwan. Taiwan has developed or preserved libraries, research institutions, and collections of art and archeological materials that make it an important repository for the impartial study of traditional Chinese culture. American scholars have a special concern to protect and develop these facilities and resources. Through such varied contacts, many Americans have come to feel a personal stake in Taiwan.

In addition, the U.S. has supplied, in military aid which includes large numbers of military advisers and equipment, most of the military apparatus of the island, and has played an important part in basic policy decisions on military matters. In other matters where we have pressed for greater political freedom for the Taiwanese and for a more democratic organization of government and administration, American advice has largely been ignored. The Nationalist army has however become largely Taiwanese, as the veterans of 1949 at the time of the retreat from the mainland have reached retirement age. For the most part, only the officers are mainland Chinese.

Taiwan is ruled by a Chinese government which was expelled from the mainland and which has never won popular support among the Taiwanese. However successful its economic program has been, this fact remains. From its island base, it has asserted a claim to continued sovereignty over all of China. If it were not for massive U.S. military and economic aid to Taiwan, and U.S. political support for Nationalist claims to China's seat in the U.N., it could not have continued to make these and other claims or to hold its present international position. The peace of the world is placed at forfeit to the conflicting claims of territorial sovereignty between two governments, one of which is emerging as a new major power, while the other enjoys its present status largely through U.S. military and economic guarantees. Eventually, unless a solution is found, the conflicting claims will be pressed to the point where the forfeit will be paid.

It is not our purpose to offer a prescription or a blueprint for a solution, but to suggest an approach which we believe may provide a basis for entirely new relationships in Asia. In order to understand the difficulties involved, it is necessary to attempt to see the problems through the eyes of each of the three parties involved: the People's Republic on the mainland, the Republic of China on Taiwan, and the United States. Both Chinese governments, while disputing each other's claim as the rightful ruler of the Chinese people, are agreed that there is only one China. The U.S., on the other hand, takes the position that there are two Chinas, namely "free China" on Taiwan and "Communist China" on the mainland, but that the only legitimate government is that on Taiwan.

As Washington Sees Taiwan

Washington arrives at this position by giving primary consideration to the present realities in the Taiwan situation. It sees on Taiwan a sovereign Chinese government to which the island was formally returned on the surrender of the Japanese in 1945. The Republic of China has ruled the island effectively for 20 years, and has held power there longer than the Communists have ruled the mainland. Washington maintains that on both legal and de facto grounds the Nationalist government must be acknowledged as the legitimate government of Taiwan and of China. The U.S. supports it as such in the United Nations and in other international organizations.

On June 27, 1950, two days after the outbreak of the Korean War, President Truman hurriedly ordered the Seventh Fleet to take position in the Taiwan Straits to isolate the island from the mainland and assure that the war did not spread southward. By this act the U.S. became committed to the support and defense of the Republic of China, a position which has been the pivot of U.S. policy in Asia ever since. This commitment reversed the declared policy at that time, which was one of refraining from extending aid to Taiwan. In 1955 President Eisenhower signed a Mutual Defense Treaty with the Republic of China by which the United States was formally committed to defend Taiwan and the Pescadores. Since May 1, 1951, the United States has had a Military Assistance Advisory Group on Taiwan to train and equip the army, navy, and air force of the Republic of China.

The government of Taiwan, though authoritarian and oligarchical, has become relatively stable and efficient. Internal subversion is not at present a serious threat. In harmony with its policy of containing communism in Asia, the United States is attempting to help Taiwan become a strong, independent nation. Both the Chinese governments, however, would argue that the disposition of Taiwan, including its people, is a purely domestic matter on which they will tolerate no outside advice or assistance, and that to entertain questions of any sort might be to imply that Chinese sovereignty (however defined) is not beyond doubt. The United States, acknowledging past failures to consider Taiwanese desires as well as present obligations to do so, and faced with the probable unwillingness of either Chinese government to do so in consultation with the United States, confronts a perplexing dilemma. If all-out support for Chiang and the Nationalist government continues indefinitely, Communist China's growing power will force an ever larger military commitment to Taiwan. If, on the other hand, the U.S. reduces its economic and military commitments to the Nationalists, it fears it will be discredited as a reliable ally in the eyes of other countries confronting the power of the People's Republic of China.

As the Republic of China Sees Taiwan

The position taken by the Republic of China (the Nationalist government) resembles in some respects that of the United States. It sees itself as the legitimate government of all of China, and its purpose is to deliver the people on the mainland from Communist rule. It fears the political and military threat posed by the Communist government in Peking, and feels the need therefore for protection beyond what it can itself provide. Consequently it has actively sought military aid from the United States and has developed a defense system of unusual strength for a government of its size.

It has set as a main objective "To exploit whatever opportunities may arise to weaken the Chinese Communist regime and to create a situation favorable to a return of the government of the Republic of China to the mainland."[16] It strives to preserve its identity and status as a sovereign nation by maintaining its position in the United Nations and other international organizations. It recognizes its dependence on the United States politically, militarily, and economically, and therefore attempts to foster the alliance which binds together the two governments. To strengthen the economy of the island and improve the fighting efficiency of its armed forces have been constant aims of the government. It seeks to cultivate and retain the loyalty of all Chinese, those on the mainland and overseas as well as those on Taiwan.

There is some basis for the belief that if Chiang Kai-shek were out of power, Peking and Taipei would resolve their differences and arrive at an amicable settlement of the Taiwan problem. It is no secret that negotiations have been going on between leaders of the two governments.[17] At various times the military forces on the island have made raids upon the mainland, not as a serious attempt at invasion but chiefly for their nuisance value. High altitude flights over the mainland are made with some regularity, using aircraft and other equipment supplied by the United States. While talk of returning to the mainland continues, there is in reality no longer any hope of doing so. As long ago as October 5, 1958, a spokesman for the Nationalist government was quoted by the London *Observer* as saying, "We haven't seriously considered invading the mainland for at least five years now. We have to keep up the pretense, of course, largely for domestic consumption—a matter of morale and discipline." It is difficult to believe that even the staunchest supporter of the Nationalist government can expect the present claim of sovereignty over all of China to survive the incumbency of Chiang Kai-shek, who is nearly 80 years old. A more pertinent question is whether revision of Tai-

16. "China (Taiwan)," Dept. of State Paper (July 1962), p. 8.
17. U.S. Dept. of State *Bulletin*, 40, No. 1032 (April 6, 1959), p. 474.

wan's relationship to China can or should be deferred until there is a successor to Chiang.

As the People's Republic Sees Taiwan

The People's Republic considers Taiwan as an integral part of China and its territory. Peking sees the United States as preventing by "armed aggression" the absorption of Taiwan by China. It is bitter because the United States, at the outbreak of the Korean War, sharply reversed its declared policy of keeping hands off and extending no aid to either side in the dispute between the Communists and the Nationalists over Taiwan. The intervention of the United States to neutralize the Taiwan Straits in June 1950 became, in Peking's eyes, a hypocritical encroachment. The Chinese Communists recall that on January 5, 1950, shortly after the Nationalist government was driven from the mainland, President Harry Truman said: "The United States government will not pursue a course which will lead to an involvement in the civil conflict in China. Similarly, the United States will not provide military aid and advice to the Chinese forces on Formosa."[18] The Peking government sees this change in United States policy at the outbreak of the Korean War as a policy of aggression toward China, and the United States as an intruder into a purely domestic matter.

The Korean War was marked by the advance of U.S. troops northward to the border of China, to which China responded with the entry of large numbers of Chinese "volunteers" into the war, leading to an eventual stalemate at parallel 38°. The Chinese sense of being wronged is heightened by their feeling that the United States, once the least offender among Western imperialist powers, has now become the chief imperialist offender by assuming vast new power commitments in Asia after the other Western nations have largely withdrawn their forces.

The mainland Chinese would have us believe that their hostility generated over the Taiwan issue is not directed against the

18. White House Press Release, January 5, 1950 (Washington, D.C.). See also remarks of Dean Acheson, January 5, 1950, as recorded in U.S. Dept. of State, *Strengthening the Forces of Freedom* (Washington, Government Printing Office, 1950), pp. 170–73.

American people but against the U.S. government. Americans however find it impossible to condone and difficult to understand the venomous attacks made upon their government by the Chinese Communists. Each side is looking at a different set of facts. Americans see themselves as benefactors of the Chinese people through the Open Door Policy, the use of Boxer indemnity money for educating Chinese students, the hospitals and colleges built by missionaries, and the assistance given China in fighting the Japanese. The Chinese see the United States as the last great exponent of colonial encroachment, and themselves as the means whereby colonialism will at last be ended. But this does not necessarily imply inevitable military conflict. From time to time China has supported negotiated settlement.

In the interview Chou En-lai granted Edgar Snow in 1960, the Chinese Premier said that at the very outset of the Chinese–United States talks in Warsaw (1955) the Chinese proposed

> that disputes between China and the United States, including the dispute between the two countries in the Taiwan region, should be settled through peaceful negotiations, without resorting to the use or threat of force. The United States blocked all news of this proposal, but China later published it.[19]

Chou claims that Secretary Dulles rejected it because he realized that the next step would be discussions on how and when United States armed forces were to withdraw from Taiwan and the Taiwan Straits.

Chou continued,

> We hold that the dispute between China and the U.S. in the Taiwan region is an international question, whereas military action between the Central Government of New China and the Chiang Kai-shek clique in Taiwan is an internal question. The U.S. has maintained that the two questions are inseparable. We hold that they can and must be separated.

Then he added these significant words:

> Since it has been possible for China and the United States to hold ambassadorial talks in Geneva and Warsaw, talks can

19. Snow, *The Other Side of the River*, p. 91.

also be held at the same time between the Central Government of China and the Chiang Kai-shek clique. The former is an international question, while the latter is an internal question. Parallel talks can be conducted and solutions reached separately.

Toward a Solution

It is evident from the divergent viewpoints presented above that what would at this time satisfy the United States as a way out of the present impasse (a withdrawal of Peking's claims to Taiwan) would be completely unacceptable to the People's Republic. On the other hand, Peking's insistence that Taiwan is a Chinese problem to be settled by Chinese is equally unsatisfactory to Washington. To offer counterproposals which are known in advance to be unacceptable to the other side will contribute nothing to the solution, but merely serve to exacerbate the antagonism of the opposing governments.

We believe that President Kennedy, in that portion of his Inaugural Address where he held out the olive branch to the "enemy," provided the formula for approaching problems such as Taiwan. He said:

> Finally, to those nations who would make themselves our adversary, we offer not a pledge but a request: that both sides begin anew the quest for peace, before the dark powers of destruction unleashed by science engulf all humanity in planned or accidental self-destruction. . . . So let us begin anew—remembering on both sides that civility is not a sign of weakness, and sincerity is always subject to proof. Let us never negotiate out of fear. But let us never fear to negotiate. Let both sides explore what problems unite us instead of laboring those problems which divide us. Let both sides for the first time formulate serious and precise proposals for the inspection and control of arms—and bring the absolute power to destroy other nations under the absolute control of all nations. Let both sides seek to invoke the wonders of science instead of its terrors. . . . Let both sides unite to heed in all corners of the earth the command of Isaiah—to "undo the heavy burdens and to let the oppressed go free."

Here is a strategy for peacemaking that stands in bold contrast to the current strategy of waging the Cold War. Let it be applied to the Taiwan issue. It embodies moral principles which if respected and practiced will bear fruit in dispelling fear, suspicion, and hate, and may ultimately create instead mutual trust, goodwill, and cooperation. Mr. Kennedy called for a fresh start, implying that the quest for a decent world must be seen as an endless series of new beginnings. Faith and patience will be required on both sides to move the mountains of resentment and hostility created by years of mutual distrust and recrimination. If any lesson has been learned from the prolonged and often tedious negotiations on disarmament and a test ban treaty, it is that no limit can be set on the number of meetings or hours of debate required in the search for acceptable answers.

Government leaders frequently reject proposals for conferences to discuss conflicting issues with an adversary on the ground that such confrontation is not timely, or that the proposals are not made in good faith, or that nothing of value would be likely to emerge from such a meeting. In a world hovering on the brink of nuclear war, it is not only timely but imperative that the search for political solutions to international problems constantly continue. Suspicion that proposals are not made in good faith should not be taken as valid basis for inaction, but should be thoroughly tested by constructive response and action. To argue that nothing of value can emerge from a proposed conference and therefore to abandon the attempt is to reject one of the most precious teachings of human experience, namely, that persistence in the face of formidable obstacles and unpromising circumstances is often rewarded with success. In diplomacy as in scientific endeavors, the "impossible" becomes possible when men believe that what needs to be done can be done.

COMMON GROUND FOR NEGOTIATION

In the pronouncements that come out of Washington and Peking can be found common principles which, if seriously pursued in practice, can provide a basis for the negotiation and settlement of the Taiwan problem. For instance, our national leaders repeatedly have assured the world that we want to live in peace with the rest of mankind, that it is not our policy to interfere in the domestic affairs of other nations, that we have no designs on the territory of others, that we are committed to a policy of nonaggression, that we believe in the principle of equality, and that we desire the highest welfare of men everywhere.

These lofty principles sound much the same as the Five Principles of Coexistence which Chou En-lai proposed at Bandung for stabilizing China's relations with other nations. These five principles are (1) mutual respect for sovereignty and territorial integrity; (2) mutual nonaggression; (3) noninterference in each other's internal affairs; (4) equality and mutual benefit; and (5) peaceful coexistence. China has based negotiation of treaties of peace and friendship with neighboring states on these principles (e.g. Burma and Pakistan). They were offered as the basis for talks about a nuclear-free Pacific peace pact. It would be easy to react negatively to China's statement of the Five Principles or her application of them, but we must recognize that abstract statements of moral or political principle cannot take the place of patient negotiation, for when great powers seek to apply agreed principles to concrete issues they see things differently and they interpret things differently. Even so, agreement on the principles can be a valuable first step if there is willingness on both sides to move on from there. Trust has been undermined by repeated instances of violated promises and treaties. It must be rebuilt, and this can be done only by taking the risk of trusting. Henry L. Stimson, in a memorandum to President Truman regarding the control of atomic bombs and U.S. relations with the Soviet Union, wrote words that need to be taken to heart by nations: "The chief lesson I have learned in a long life is that the only way you can make a man trustworthy is to trust him; and the surest way to make him untrustworthy is to distrust him and show your distrust."[20]

We believe that China and the United States, through talks at high level, should seek to discover common ground on which the negotiation of the Taiwan dispute can proceed. To take the position in advance that Taiwan is not negotiable is to perpetuate the stalemate. To propose fixed or rigid solutions in advance is

20. Henry L. Stimson and McGeorge Bundy, *On Active Service in Peace and War* (New York, Harper, 1948), p. 644.

to place roadblocks in the way of the kind of communication essential for preparing both parties in their search for solutions. Efforts must be made to clear up misunderstandings on both sides. The "curtain of ignorance" must be removed, and Americans and Chinese must be permitted to see and know each other's country after 15 years of isolation.

President Johnson has at various times proposed a formula for dealing with conflict situations by quoting words from the prophecy of Isaiah, "Come now, let us reason together." In this we believe is to be found the spirit and the method for dealing with the differences that divide the People's Republic and the United States on Taiwan and other issues. For Americans or Chinese to question the possibility of a rational approach and settlement of this problem is not only to postpone the benefits that could accrue to China and the U.S.A. from friendly co-operation. It is to prolong the threat of nuclear war inherent in this critical tension area of East Asia. Nations, like men, need not remain the way they are, and do not, as witness the current friendly Japanese-American or German-American relations in contrast to the hostility of the war years. The discovery of common interests brought about improved relations. The common interests of the United States and China, as President Kennedy suggested, may be found in grappling together with the problems of ignorance, hunger, disease, poverty, and the scourge of war.

Recognizing that there is no simple solution to the problem of Taiwan, the writers of this report are nevertheless convinced that public discussion should take into account various alternatives. Settlement of the issue of Taiwan is one key to peace in East Asia. It may be the key to peace for all mankind. If the United States were to decide that an attempt to resolve the Taiwan problem should now be made, and if it should repeat the request in President Kennedy's Inaugural Address "that both sides begin anew the quest for peace," it might quietly approach the heads of both governments, on the mainland and on Taiwan, and express its desire for talks aimed at a peaceful settlement of all problems that divide them. Washington might inform Peking of its readiness to respond to Chou En-lai's proposal made at the Bandung Conference "to sit down and enter into negotiations with the United States Government to discuss existing disputes between the two countries."[21] New initiatives to break the present stalemate might facilitate direct negotiations.

SOME SPECIFIC ISSUES

Because of the dilemmas posed by Taiwan's present status, should we not consider the possibility of an international negotiating commission, under U.N. auspices if possible, on which both contending governments would be represented, but on which no group alone could determine the procedure and outcome? There is an obvious basis for the appointment of such a commission, in the present inability and unwillingness of the two contestants to work out a settlement among themselves. Their conflict over Taiwan is a clear and major threat to world peace, and as such is the proper concern of other powers and of the U.N. which, if activated, might encourage direct negotiation.

The issue of Taiwan's status will become a matter of heated controversy if and when the members of the United Nations vote favorably on the resolution which has been before the General Assembly each year since 1961: "The Restoration of the Lawful Rights of the People's Republic of China in the United Nations." The success of this resolution would inflict a psychological defeat on the Nationalist government by taking away its seat in the U.N. The Peking government would then be in a place to press in the U.N. its claims for jurisdiction over Taiwan. Since there is a high probability that this resolution will win the support of the requisite majority of U.N. members within the next few years, its effect on the rights and welfare of the people on Taiwan becomes of practical importance. Under the U.S.-protected regime of Chiang Kai-shek the Taiwanese have enjoyed few rights. How would a changed situation affect them?

The so-called "two Chinas" proposal by which both the Chinese People's Republic and the Republic of China would be members of the United Nations has never been on the agenda of the U.N. General Assembly, but was articulated by the Foreign Minister of Ireland in his speech of December 8, 1964. If both countries were to be considered as "successor" states, Taiwan would keep

21. Snow, *The Other Side of the River*, p. 89.

VOTING IN THE U.N. GENERAL ASSEMBLY
ON CHINESE REPRESENTATION

(Vote on "Restoration of Lawful Rights,"
⅔ of yeas and nays required)

	Yes	No	Abstention
1961	37	48	19
1962	42	56	12
1963	41	57	12

its seat in the General Assembly and Peking would be offered seats in both the Assembly and the Security Council. Since both Peking and Taipei reject any thought of a "two Chinas" solution, it would be difficult to gain support for it at the United Nations.

From time to time suggestions have been made that Taiwan might be brought under the protection of some sort of U.N. trusteeship. Since the U.N. Charter specifically says "The trusteeship system shall not apply to territories which have become members of the United Nations" (Article 78), the Nationalist government would have to give up not only its claim to authority over the mainland but also its sovereignty over Taiwan. Furthermore, a trusteeship is not envisaged by the Charter as a permanent solution but rather as a step in the "progressive development toward self-government or independence." It could be argued that the U.N. is not equipped to undertake the huge administrative responsibility for a trusteeship on behalf of 12 million people. (The only precedents for a United Nations administration have been the short-term arrangements for the transfer of sovereignty in Libya in 1949–51 and in West Irian in 1962–63; each of these transitional administrations involved reliance on local administrative personnel committed to the transfer of authority.) The People's Republic of China has denounced trusteeship for Taiwan as completely unacceptable.

If the political prospects for an entirely separate status for the present government of Taiwan seem remote, the possibility of negotiation between Taiwan and Peking regarding Taiwanese autonomy within *one China* seems only slightly less difficult. Even so, in offering to negotiate a one China solution the parties concerned would be in a position to seek to preserve both fundamental human rights and a measure of freedom for the Taiwanese people within the larger context of association with the mainland.

GUIDING PRINCIPLES AND POLICIES

To sum up, we see no practical or acceptable alternative to acknowledging that the People's Republic of China is the government of China, that the Republic of China actually is no more than the U.S.-protected government of Taiwan, and that both of these governments agree that "Taiwan is a part of China." We suggest that this point of agreement might become the basis of broader agreement. This suggestion is not likely to be received with enthusiasm either in Peking or in Taiwan, since both governments claim sovereignty over the territory of the other. Nevertheless we believe that acknowledgment of the realities of the present situation may provide the best point from which to begin the attempt to build a better situation. This means that the real government of China should occupy China's seat in the United Nations. It means that the question of the status of Taiwan in the U.N. and elsewhere may no longer be linked to illusory claims of mainland sovereignty long since lost, but must be the subject of negotiation based upon present realities.

If a solution were to be approached in this way, there would be many difficulties before it could be accomplished. The People's Republic might not accept its place in the United Nations without a final settlement of the status of Taiwan. The Republic of China might not be willing to accept or apply for a U.N. General Assembly seat as the government of Taiwan. On the other hand, if the People's Republic took China's seat and the Republic of China applied for a Taiwan seat, the application could be vetoed by any member of the Security Council, which then would include not only the People's Republic but also the U.S.S.R.

In the face of these uncertainties, it seems to us that the prudent and moral course for the United States is to move forward from the present stalemate guided by the conviction that peaceful solutions can often be found in the most unpromising situations if sought with persistence and understanding based on knowledge, insight, and goodwill. Where questions of political status and

57

authority are in dispute partisan feelings should not prevent clarity on the actual circumstances. In line with these convictions, we believe that the U.S. should accept the People's Republic as the rightful occupant of China's seat in the United Nations and should maintain consistently that any disputes over sovereignty or other problems affecting relations between the People's Republic and the nationalist government on Taiwan should be the subject of negotiation.

The purpose of this policy would be the peaceful stabilization of Taiwan–Mainland–U.S. relationships and the ultimate withdrawal of the U.S. Seventh Fleet from the straits of Taiwan by the agreement of all parties concerned. As an encouragement to the successful completion of these negotiations, the United States would support the government on Taiwan during the period of negotiations, having affirmed in principle the desirability of ultimate withdrawal of military support as soon as political understanding has been reached or other security arrangements made which will better serve the purposes of peace and good relationships in the area than an alien and provocative fleet of warships.

THE TRAGEDY OF DIVIDED NATIONS

The China–Taiwan issue is not unique in the modern world. Among the greatest tragedies of the twentieth century are those of divided nations—China, Germany, Korea, Vietnam, and we might add, even Ireland and the split between India and Pakistan. It is futile to try to apportion blame for such division; in the conflict of ideologies this has often seemed the least objectionable way out. It is a solution however which is stained with human tragedy—families divided, hatred fanned, development frustrated, communications throttled. The guilt for this tragedy lies heavily on all of us. Once a country has been divided, however, and its two parts have followed different paths of growth for a generation or more, reunion becomes more and more difficult and the division may simply have to be accepted as a social fact. Organic reunion of Britain and the United States, for instance, would have been enormously difficult at any time after the Revolution and is now virtually impossible; nevertheless the lack of union imposes no hostilities or tensions today.

The authors of this paper find themselves torn between two

opposing sentiments—one a strong sympathy with the Chinese and other divided peoples in their search for unity, the other a painful awareness that obsession with unity can be enormously costly in terms of human welfare. The memory of our own Civil War makes both the passion for unity and its high cost poignantly vivid in the American mind. On the other hand, the success of our relations with Canada, passing from counterrevolution and war to disarmament and cooperative coexistence in a few generations, suggests to us that in this case unity would not have been worth the cost to either side.

The welfare of mankind demands that we concentrate on making all divisions and boundaries between states unimportant or even beneficial rather than attempt to reunite what may have become alien social bodies. Once out of the womb, a child can never be reunited with its mother; it can only love her. Political births may be monstrous and arbitrary, but if they result in viable children which grow into a different way of life from their parents, reunion after a certain point may be too difficult to be worth the cost. We do not know whether the relations of Taiwan and Communist China have reached this point; we cannot however exclude this possibility.

6. SECURITY IN EAST ASIA

In this paper we have argued that there are new policy approaches toward China that the United States can and should take, which would be based on encouraging confidence and trust rather than on threat and counterthreat. We have viewed the effects of these proposals in the context of a developing world community through the United Nations, and we have considered the implications for Taiwan and our commitments there.

It is only fair that we be expected to deal with the security implications of our proposals. What would be the effect in Asia if we withdrew the Seventh Fleet, reduced our Asian bases, and sought to deal with China and the power problems around the periphery of China (India, Malaysia, Burma, Thailand, Laos, Cambodia, Vietnam, Taiwan, Korea) not in terms of military might but in terms of goodwill and confidence in the effective authority of the world community? Entirely apart from ultimate judgments as to the morality or efficacy of arms, this is a fair question, for the fact is that our world bristles with arms, the U.S. is the largest single military power, and any sharp reduction in U.S. armed strength will inevitably alter the relationships of power throughout the area affected by the reduction. Our proposals for withdrawal of U.S. military strength from Taiwan and the Taiwan Straits invite the question: Would this not lead to invasion and control from the mainland?

With only slight variations, the same question confronts us when we think of a withdrawal from Vietnam or from South Korea. These questions point toward a still more basic question: How can a genuine security system be achieved in Asia to replace the uncertain security of nationalistic military power?

First, let us consider what security needs would be likely to remain in East Asia if U.S. reliance on military power were sharply reduced. Admittedly this depends to some extent on one's assessment of the objectives and character of the Chinese Communist government. How aggressive or potentially aggressive is it? The best-informed people disagree on the answer. Our own assessment is that China clearly wants to include Tibet, Sinkiang, and Taiwan under its control and to exercise a degree of influence in North Korea and North Vietnam. These are areas which have traditionally been part of or closely attached to the Chinese empire, whenever in the past the central government was strong, as it certainly is now. In this context, the forcible Chinese reannexation of Tibet, the heavy hand of the Communist state in Sinkiang, and Chinese moves to increase their influence in Korea and Vietnam, unjustified as they may be in American eyes, may be understood more accurately as internecine interference and intervention than as traditional aggression. The Chinese action against India was clearly the outright invasion of another country, but the case was not nearly as straightforward as might appear, and the Chinese claim to parts of the disputed areas, as compared to India's, are plausible. China will most likely continue to give assistance to Communist groups involved in "wars of liberation" in other countries, especially along its own borders, and its leaders clearly believe that eventually the world as a whole will be Communist. This aggressive threat of covert conspiracy is less a danger to neighbors whose economic and political position is strong. In contrast, military dictators and implacable poverty invite subversion.

These actions and beliefs do not in themselves mean, however, that China wants to conquer the world, or even East Asia, by military force, or that the only workable policy for the United States is to counter with force, hostility, and "containment." Such a policy has not succeeded either in solving the problems posed by a vigorous Communist Chinese state in East Asia or in ensuring the security of the other nations of the area. Where outright force has been used in an effort to counter communism, notably in Korea and Vietnam, the results have been tragically unsuccessful and have carried with them in addition the dreadful risk of global war.

It is our view that security basically resides in the confidence of the people, and that no government can command confidence if it must rely on alien armed might. Although the people of the United States have sincerely believed that the deployment and use of armed might in Asia has made freedom and democracy more secure and communism less viable, exactly the reverse is the case. The threat which most Americans now believe the Chinese Communists are posing would be greatly lessened by the reduction of the present reliance on U.S. military power and by greater reliance on the measures we have proposed. If American proposals for gradual military withdrawal were to be suggested in principle by the United States as a first step in negotiation toward a resolution of the problem, it might reasonably be matched by a Chinese Communist undertaking to abstain from every kind of military action in the Taiwan area as well as in the larger area of East Asia where American forces are also deployed. There is at least a reasonable prospect though no guarantee that such a bargaining exchange would make sense to the Chinese Communists, especially if the groundwork could be laid through private discussions rather than through public negotiation. The success of an arrangement of this sort, and the degree to which it could in fact bring security or stability to the area, would depend to a considerable extent on the government of China. Its basic attitude could be better tested and its long-term objectives could be more accurately assessed if a negotiated settlement were to be attempted than is now the case when the validity of the worst fears of the United States about China is taken for granted. No one really knows how China would respond to a sustained U.S. effort to reach a peaceful settlement through negotiation. However, even if China responded entirely negatively the United States would be in a better position having tried to negotiate and China's neighbors would not be worse off because the effort had been made.

The interests and needs of the other nations of East Asia must also be considered. The exchange of the present military threats and guerrilla warfare for a set of mutual undertakings between the United States and China to avoid the use of force would offer most of these countries a very much more attractive basis for security than now exists. The weak new nations in the buffer zone along China's borders: the two Koreas, the two Vietnams, Laos, and Cambodia can only continue to suffer from their present role as violent centers for U.S.–China conflict. Chinese efforts to ensure that China is not surrounded by countries which harbor U.S. military bases or act as staging grounds for military forces aimed against China is understandable. The United States feels the same way about Cuba. It is reasonable to conclude that China wants security so that it can develop its economy, rather than territorial expansion, although it also wants to ensure that its neighbors are friendly, or perhaps even under its influence. The security of the small countries along the Chinese borders can better be protected against Chinese pressures through U.S.–Chinese agreement, or through international supervision, than by force. None of the other countries of East Asia, from Japan to Pakistan, could withstand a military attack by China or by the United States. All of them stand to profit from the successful substitution of negotiation for force as a basis for security; many of them, especially Japan, are anxious to increase their trade with the China market. Even if efforts to find peaceful solutions are abortive, the loss would not be greater than if present preoccupation with military solutions is allowed to run its tragic course, and our moral position would be far stronger than if we refuse to negotiate.

Operating with this new definition of security, we are confident that the United Nations as a laboratory for a new type of diplomacy can, despite its present weaknesses, continue to develop machinery and techniques for managing problems such as those of East and Southeast Asia. In any negotiations, the extension of U.N. responsibilities, within the scope of available resources, can be a step toward world order. The precise forms of U.N. participation in a settlement or of some U.N. "presence" in the area will emerge only from extended negotiation which includes China. The goal should be to seek a settlement that will advance the quest for world community.

All thoughts about military and security problems in Asia have had to be reviewed since the Chinese exploded a nuclear bomb. Not only does this achievement alter many aspects of the strategic and policy situation in the area, but it threatens to disrupt the nuclear test ban treaty and makes it essential for China to be intimately involved in any future discussion of the use and restriction of nuclear weapons. This development may indeed present a further opportunity for negotiation. China is still far from being able to challenge the United States in the nuclear field; the pressing need for rapid development of the Chinese economy puts a further premium, from the Chinese point of view, on the absence of war and on avoiding a nuclear arms race. China would have much to gain from a nuclear-free Pacific, or a nuclear-free East Asia, and has indeed already made such a proposal. A nuclear ban might be worked out in association with other agreements involving the withdrawal or scaling down of present American and Chinese military efforts and support in the area, as discussed above, or it might be negotiated separately. But the Chinese nuclear test may now have put before both China and the United States the possibility of genuine and mutually advantageous concessions to each other as the price of mutual security in East Asia which has so long, so tragically, and so dangerously been lacking. A policy based on hostility and force has brought neither security nor stability. Instead it has heightened the common peril. When communication is resumed between China and the United States, when negotiating machinery is available, and when America is willing to abandon nonrecognition and ostracism of China in favor of an attempt at resolving differences by methods short of war, we may expect the Chinese response to be more constructive than we have had any right to expect during the past 15 years of unrelieved mutual hostility. Even though solid results would remain uncertain and improvements would come only slowly and with difficulty, a policy based on achieving mutually beneficial goals is a more promising approach to security in East Asia than we have yet tried.

Such a policy could fail, but so can military-based policies as we have seen. In either case there are risks to be run. The important thing is not so much to become lost in assessing the risks as to grasp the positive and constructive opportunities that could be opened up for all of the people of Asia by success in negotiating a general settlement with China.

EPILOGUE

The great object before us from which we should never be deterred is the achievement of a world security community—a world in which "each shall live under his own vine and his own fig tree and none shall make them afraid," a world in which threats and counterthreats no longer rule the relations of men and nations. A security community is not an idle dream; over sections of the world it already exists. In Scandinavia, among the English-speaking countries, recently in Western Europe, and among the socialist states, groups of nations have emerged within which war becomes increasingly improbable even to the point where it becomes unthinkable; war is no longer a factor in the behavior of these nations toward one another.

Asia, alas, is not a security community, and violence and the threat of violence are a commonplace in the relations of its states. The great question in Asia is how can we set in motion a process that will bring about a security community? We look for a learning process, by which more and more people, both leaders and followers, widen their horizons of concern, learn to think long-sightedly in making decisions, to appraise accurately the full results of their actions, and to create and support those institutions which can achieve their ends. It is by growth of this kind that existing security communities have been built, and it is only by a similar growth that a security community can be built in strife-torn Asia.

If what we look for is a learning process, who then are the teachers? We ask ourselves, as Americans, how is our own country learning or teaching? In our relations with Russia, we see a slow but persistent learning process going on, and there is room for a modest optimism that if this growth continues we may yet achieve a security community. In Asia we neither learn nor teach security in community. Despite the constructive social and economic development efforts of the United States in several Asian countries, our presence in Asia is increasingly a presence of threat and counterthreat. We are teaching the Asians not peace, but war. This we are eager to reverse, and we plead with our own country-men to examine in their hearts and minds the role of America in Asia, and to ask whether it is leading toward or away from the security community we all seek.

The matter is desperately urgent, and the time is late. Asia is well along the road that leads only to destruction, a destruction that may pull down the whole world. A nuclear arms race is already on: witness the explosion in 1964 of a nuclear device by the People's Republic of China and the announcement early in 1965 by Indonesia that it is working toward the development of atomic weapons. Polaris submarines stalk the Asian waters. Japan could easily achieve an independent nuclear capability, and if the arms race continues may be strongly tempted to do so. The same is true for India. This is a road to suicide; it kills the hope of human betterment.

But who, our readers may ask, are we—a handful of Quakers, speaking only for ourselves—to set ourselves up as teachers, with our limited knowledge and experience? The question is a fair one, and we speak out humbly, with an acute sense of our limitations. But speak out we must. We believe there is an inward teacher, to which through our lives we have tried to listen and to which we believe all people everywhere can attend. By this inward teacher we are convinced that there is a way of death, and a way of life. The way of death is the way of threat and violence, hatred and malevolence, rigid ideology and obsessive nationalism. This way is all too easy to find. The way of life is harder to find, it is uphill, and takes hard work of mind and body and, even more difficult, purification of spirit. Neither rulers, nor parties, nor nations, nor ideologies, nor religions can command the legitimate loyalties of men unless they serve the way of life. Nothing but the truth has divine right. Hard as it is to find, we believe the way of life can and must be found, and we urge all people everywhere to dedicate their lives to its finding.

BIBLIOGRAPHY

BARNETT, A. DOAK. *Communist China and Asia: A Challenge to American Policy.* New York, Vintage V-185 (paper), 1960. 560 pp. Thorough introduction by a leading China expert.

————, *Communist China: Continuing Revolution.* Headline Series No. 153. Foreign Policy Association, May–June 1962. 60 pp. A summary of Mao's domestic and foreign policies.

————, *Communist China in Perspective.* New York, Praeger, 1962.

BUSS, CLAUDE A. *The People's Republic of China.* Princeton, Van Nostrand, 1962. Paper. 190 pp. The author, a well-known Stanford professor of history, traces the origins, rise to power, achievements, and failures of the Chinese Communists.

CLUBB, O. EDMUND. *20th Century China.* New York, Columbia University Press, 1964. 470 pp. China's recent history, with emphasis on the impact of communism, by a former foreign service officer who was in North China in 1949.

COHEN, ARTHUR A. *The Communism of Mao Tse-tung.* Chicago, University of Chicago Press, 1964. 210 pp. A carefully documented evaluation of Mao's contribution to Communist thought and practice.

FAIRBANK, JOHN K. *The United States and China.* New York, Viking Press C-108 (paper), 1958 ed. 348 pp. Essential background for the present situation. A standard work by a leading Harvard specialist. An excellent introduction to modern China.

FITZGERALD, C. P. *The Chinese View of Their Place in the World.* New York, Oxford University Press, 1964. 72 pp. Traces the connection between China's past and present pretensions to world leadership.

KUO PING-CHIA. *China New Age and New Outlook.* Penguin Books (S-179), 1960. A stimulating and challenging analysis of the Chinese revolution and of the first decade of the Communist regime by a well-known Chinese historian, now at Southern Illinois University.

LI, CHOH-MING, ed. *Industrial Development in Communist China*. A special issue (No. 17, 1964) of the periodical *China Quarterly* (London), which has also been reprinted in book form.

MANCALL, MARK, ed. *Formosa Today*. New York, Praeger, 1964. 171 pp. Essays by 13 experts giving a broad picture of Taiwan and the Chiang regime today.

NEWMAN, ROBERT P. *The Recognition of Communist China*. New York, Macmillan, 1961.

SNOW, EDGAR. *The Other Side of the River: Red China Today*. New York, Random House, 1961. 810 pp. A long, sympathetic account of the Communist regime by almost the only U.S. journalist with recent access to Mao and Chou. Snow interviewed top Communist leaders after the Long March and more recently in Peking.

TSOU TANG. *America's Failure in China 1941–50*. Chicago, University of Chicago Press, 1963. 614 pp. A solid, documented treatment of U.S. policy toward China in the decade 1940–50.

WHITNEY, NORMAN. "The Same Clothes Will Not Always Serve." Philadelphia, American Friends Service Committee, 1965. Paper. A study guide including supplementary material on *A New China Policy* for the use of adult education courses and groups.

ZAGORIA, DONALD S. *The Sino-Soviet Conflict, 1956–1961*. Princeton, Princeton University Press, 1962. Detailed study of how the Sino-Soviet rift came about.

China Today. Philadelphia, American Friends Service Committee, 1965. Paper. 79 pp. Essays dealing with the history, philosophy, political organization, economic development, foreign policy, and family life of present-day China, reprinted from *The Political Quarterly*, (Edinburgh) (July–September 1964).